Bubble
Girl

An Irreverent Journey of Faith

KATHRYN BANAKIS

CHALICE
PRESS

ST. LOUIS, MISSOURI

Cover art: Photo of author
Cover design: Elizabeth Wright

Visit www.chalicepress.com

10 9 8 7 6 5 4 3 2 1   13 14 15 16 17 18 19

Print: 9780827202900   EPUB: 9780827202917   EPDF: 9780827202924

Library of Congress Cataloging–in–Publication Data available upon request.

Contents

Acknowledgments

Thanks to...

Brad Lyons, Russ White, and the entire Chalice Press team for taking this project on.

Rebecca Bowman Woods, Brandon Gilvin, and Christian Piatt for seeing possibility throughout the editing process. Your guidance, good humor, and encouragement were pure gift.

The Lilly Endowment, the Fund for Theological Education, the Youth Theological Initiative, the Institute of Sacred Music at Yale, Berkeley Divinity School at Yale, and the Turley Foundation for supporting my theological education.

The faith communities who have (perhaps unwittingly) raised me, and the small groups who have prayed me into adulthood.

Ray Waddle, Jason Peno, T.J. Altman, Chris Meserole, Grace Han, Phyllis Tickle, Shannon Craigo-Snell, Anne Howard, Nora Gallagher, Tricia Crisafulli, Cotton Fite, Meghan Young, Eva, Emily Breunig, Emily Jones, Danielle Tumminio Hansen, Becky Strehlow, and Jeannette DeFriest for their thoughtful reading of drafts in whole or part and insights into how to move it from concept to reality. Any errors are mine.

My host of fairy godparents in the faith who have gone before me and beckoned me to follow: Sandy and David Stayner, Steve Huber, Drew Bunting, Julie Kelsey, Frannie Hall-Kieschnick, Emilie Townes, Nora Tubbs Tisdale, Char Heeg, Melissa Wiginton, Julaine Kammrath, Davis Fisher, Matthew Dutton-Gillette, Jaime and Peyton McElroy, Greta Getlein.

And my family for being wonderfully game for all of the adventures. I am so blessed to have been given to you.

A Note on Truthiness

The stories contained in this book are true, but some names and facts have been changed in the interest of privacy or blips in my memory. Any and all errors are my fault, my fault, my most grievous fault.

Foreword

I love it that one of my clergy friends signs her emails with this quote from Audrey Hepburn:

> "I love people who make me laugh. I honestly think it's the thing I like most, to laugh. It cures a multitude of ills. It's probably the most important thing in a person."

Hepburn's quote is great in itself, but what tickles me is that it comes into my inbox from a woman of the cloth. There's too much about religion that's not funny—at least not in a good way.

So that's why I'm downright delighted with *Bubble Girl*. And I bet you will be too. In fact, you might want to speedread the rest of this Foreword, because life is too short to put off laughter.

But if you are staying with me for a few more minutes, let me tell you a little more about why I'm so delighted with this book and with this author.

The first thing to say is that this book matters. Now I believe that Forewords to books ought to touch upon the context in which a particular book matters at a particular time, so I will say a word about that.

Kat Banakis's book matters because it's not just her story: it's our story, and the story of what it means to be a person of faith (or not) at this moment in time. This is a deeply personal memoir, but one that holds up a mirror for all of us to see ourselves, in all our glory and warts. And this the story of the church, which Kat calls "a shiny, lumpy crabapple of an institution" (that's in the line when she's explaining why she loves the church and wants to work in it as a priest). Kat gives me hope for that crabapple.

Kat's book matters because she dares to speak the truth (in love, of course) about what happens when one human being comes into contact with the institution we call the church. She shows us the church, not as we have might have known it or seen it once upon a time, or as it would like to be known or seen, but rather the church as it is and as it is changing (or groaning in expectation, the apostle Paul might say) in the twenty-first century.

Kat says that we make church not for reasons of family tradition or tribal orthodoxy but because of felt need (childcare) and circumstance (new in town, need friends). She shows good church and bad church, but most importantly she shows us real church.

As a member of the "first globals" generation, Kat gives us a glimpse of what the changing church might look like in the years ahead. It's worth the view. Kat nudges us into the change with her questions, her keen insight, her fresh wisdom, and her good humor, just at this moment in time when we all need to grasp the change in which we find ourselves.

This change, Diana Butler Bass says in her newest book *Christianity After Religion: The End of Church and the Birth of a New Spiritual Awakening*, (Harper, 2012) is not just about change within in the church, but change throughout the culture. Bass says that we are in the midst of a social transformation in which we see in a new generation of spiritual seekers "travelling new paths of meaning, exploring new ways to live their lives, experiencing a new sense of authenticity and wonder, and practicing new forms of community that address global concerns of human flourishing." Kat is one of those practitioners.

Kat's book matters to me because I spend my days working with young faith leaders who are taking a critical look at the way we do church, and imagining new ways to gather as community and tell our stories and care for one another and the planet. These young leaders of The Beatitudes Society are committed to growing new kinds of churches that are welcoming, inclusive, prayerful, engaged in the needs of the neighborhood and the needs of the global human family, and not boring. Kat tells the story of the church these leaders (along with the rest of us) have inherited, and she begins to paint the picture of the church she and her generation will create.

Now I know that lots of people aren't interested in church—the latest Pew Research poll (July 2012) showed that a whopping 19% of Americans check "None" when asked to name their religion—but I'd be willing to wager a bet that this book might be one that a None would like. That's because Kat tells us, with keen perception, unabashed honesty, and deep intelligence, what it's like to be human, what it's like to feel alone, what it's like to be connected to someone close and Something Bigger (capitals mine, not hers.) She offers no pat answers and no TMI dirty laundry sharing, just a great conversation. It's a conversation worth sharing. I can imagine this book jump-starting great conversations in book clubs, youth groups, and maybe even families, especially families whose children have grown up to check "None."

So here's a list of delights I found in *Bubble Girl*:

- She salts her personal stories with a bit of theology, church history, and church practice, and covers topics like God, Jesus, Baptism, Sacraments, Crucifixion, Resurrection, Biblical Interpretation, and Prayer, and of course, her own wrestling with ordination. I hesitate to name such topics in the Foreword, because I don't want to tip you off to the learning that will take place while you are laughing. Think Stephen Colbert or Jon Stewart. This book is a brilliant introduction to the history and practices of Christianity.

- She gives us some fresh vocabulary for churchy things. A sacrament, for example, is "a public moment of transparency." Not bad. Church is not St. Augustine's "heaven full of saints and sanctity and all the sopranos singing Alleluias in key all day long" nor is it polite, pristine, and pretty. It's "real people, trying to find community, trying our best to raise energetic children to be kind adults, trying to learn what it will mean to have a good death, singing songs off-key, enacting the sacraments, learning to forgive one another because we're still the same people coming back together week after week after week, and in the mist of all of this, hoping to know God." That's the church we're looking for.

- She describes the saints as "the ones who have gone before us, rooting for the church on earth to keep on trucking."

- She nails pie-in-the-sky Christianity with her treatment of the "superhero" version of Jesus that sees Jesus as the "ultimate roll of duct tape to patch up creation."

- She shows us the compassion that is at the heart of Christianity (and all the great religions of the world) in showing us a Christianity that hasn't been capturing the headlines lately, one that looks like Jesus: daring, inclusive, enthused, welcoming, a little ragged.

- She dares to name at least one sacrament as "territorial," but I'll leave it to you to find out which one.

- She makes hilarious puns smack in the middle of clarifying theological commentary, and she has more fun with footnotes than should be legal, as in this declaration about good and evil: "He doesn't vacuum us up, up, and away from them, which sometimes totally sucks because then we're still stuck in our earthly lives." The footnote: "Pun intended." Or there's her footnote on Calvin's doctrine of predestination: "Oh, I know Theodore Beza and others drove home double-predestination, and it really started with Augustine who waffled on it, but we both know that Calvin gets the credit historically." Or the footnote on the Holy Spirit, aka, in Greek, *parakletos*: "Pear-uh-clee-tos. My divinity school's (surprisingly competitive) soccer team was called the Pair a Cleats. Groan."

o   She tells the truth about what it's like to be a stranger in a strange place, i.e., church: she enters a church coffee hour, the new kid on the block, wishing she were Wolf Blitzer—you have to read this— and she ends up admitting that what she wants in that coffee hour is what we all want from church: "I want people to want to talk to me, to feel an intimacy with me and want to connect. Or maybe, what I really want is to be known." Of course. Don't we all want to be known?

That brings me to her title, Bubble Girl. Where does that come from? It comes from a place we know, but a place that I haven't seen named so poignantly and pointedly before. It's about that moment we don't talk about: "I'll make a joke that flops...or try to launch a church initiative...and a Plexiglas wall descends between me and the people I was just talking to... loneliness arrives like a quarantine vessel, and I am Bubble Girl, alone and isolated in the midst of them." There is a Bubble Girl in all of us, and Kat has the temerity to name this, and to allow us to chuckle as we recognize what's really real in her life and our own.

In the end, she learns that she can bring her whole self into the life of faith, and into leadership in the church, even when she is "a hot mess of mascara and snot"; she knows herself to be accepted, to be home, to find her end in her beginning. Think Tillich, or Dorothy back in Kansas, or T.S. Eliot.

Isn't this what we all need to learn? Kat Banakis is one fine teacher, mascara, snot, and all.

The Rev. Anne S. Howard
Executive Director
The Beatitudes Society

Introduction

Like many a modern American coming of age story, this story begins with a road trip. The year was 2009, when the economy was in shambles but gas prices were still cheap. My youngest sister and I were on our way from Chicago to Northern California where a graduate student sublet apartment, replete with cast-off furniture and windows that didn't close, awaited me.

Wait. Scratch that. I have to pick up my sister first. Okay, this story begins like many a modern American coming of age story, with a road trip. The year was 2009, when the economy was in shambles but gas prices were still cheap. I had just graduated from divinity school in New Haven, Connecticut, and was moving to Northern California. My youngest sister, still in high school, couldn't find a summer job (see note on economy) and agreed to copilot me through the plains of Nebraska and Wyoming. So I packed up my grandmother's twenty-year-old Honda Accord that, after three years of living on the streets of New Haven looked...like something that had spent three years living on the streets of New Haven. The hood and roof had been attacked by bionic acorns and other denting forces. The wheel openings bore rust spots. The antenna could only be raised or lowered manually. She was a great car, but not a great multi-tasker. She could accelerate, blow cool air, or play the radio—but only one at a time.

I stopped in Chicago to pick up my sister, let the car rest, and to make the obligatory visit to relatives.

So—hold on, I need to explain the why of said road trip.

This story begins, like many a modern American coming of age story, at my meeting with the bishop's office, at which they laid out their expectations for my discernment period prior to ordination to the priesthood in the Episcopal Church. You know the one—that meeting after you're approved for Round One* of the ordination process, but before Round Two.** It's that big session when you meet with a representative from the bishop's ordaining committee and the bishop's staff person to find out your marching orders for the coming months and years.

Oh…right…that would only be a familiar coming of age story if it were 1809, and I were a boy, and all New England institutions of higher ed were, in fact, seminaries. Okay, so an industrial and gender revolution later, I'm sitting in the bishop's office in Connecticut, an old mansion built back in the 1800s at least, and the committee member, the bishop's staffer, my supervisor from the church where I've been interning for two years, and I are around a huge wooden table right out of Camelot. It's early January in New England. The sun is bouncing off the snow, through the stained-glass windows in the parlor.

Many people and years have led up to this meeting. Ordination in the Episcopal tradition is always a combination of a person sensing a "call" to ordained ministry and then a series of local communities publicly affirming that they sense the same direction for that person and see said person as a minister, too. First is the local congregation, then a regional body, then a whole range of people at divinity school—administrators and teachers and internship supervisors and classmates—then finally the bishop's advisory committee, and the bishop(s). It's a series of sound checks. *Do you hear what I hear? Yep, good to proceed.*

The ordination process is also regional, with each region setting its own rules and processes and clergy quota. I lived in Washington, D.C., when I began the process, but that region hit its quota and stopped accepting "newbies." So I moved to Connecticut to both attend divinity school and establish residency at a church in the Connecticut region to start the process there. It was sort of like a political hopeful might buy a house in the next town over to be within a different ward. Now, though, I am much delayed in the process when compared to my classmates and friends from other regions and denominations. It's right off into ordained ministry positions for many of them—the ones who stand too close in conversation and pet my arm when we talk; those who have adopted British accents and PBS costume drama attire (though they grew up in suburban Atlanta); and even the people who are late to class because they were slain by the Spirit in the cafeteria. (*Hate it when that happens.*)

The four of us at the knights of the round table do a quick review of all the classes I've taken, my internships at the church and as a chaplain at an

---

* Postulancy.
** Candidacy.

inner-city hospital, the seven written exams administered by the Episcopal Church, and the Shakespeare or Bible quotes quiz in which I had to say whether a quote was an aphorism from the Bard or a quote from the Good Book (a test that would have been equally appropriate for an English major *or* a religion major), the mental and physical tests I've undergone, and my extensive criminal background check.

"Well," the bishop's representative says brightly, "Everything seems to be in order here. We'll have some more oral exams and periodic interviews of course, but you're in great shape. We should be on schedule, God willing and the people consenting,* for a 2012 priesting."**

"No sooner?" I ask.

"Now Kat," the committee representative answers patiently, "We've been very clear with you about the process. This period is critical for you and us to mutually discern if ordination to the priesthood is the right thing for you."

Really, by the Connecticut region's rules and regs, things can't go any faster. I know that. But there are always apocryphal stories of people being fast tracked, and maybe, just maybe, I could be one of them. No dice.

I am still disappointed. It's like when you're driving on the kind of highway that has hundreds of miles between exits, and you really have to go, but it's only ten more miles and so you self-talk and avoid thinking of waterfalls until you get to the exit. Then you pull off and follow the exit road deeper and deeper into an unknown place. Minutes and meadows pass and finally you come upon a concrete slab with rusted gas pumps and a hand-lettered marquis sign that reads "$ .89/gl." And what had been self-talk to endure the last bit becomes internal organ ache and despair.

Maybe you know something of what I was feeling. Maybe you're familiar with the doubt around a sunken opportunity cost: three years of school and unemployment passed. You also might know what it is to be young enough that three more years feels like a *very* long time to pour into a career path that might not work out. Perhaps you know what it is to wonder if you've made a horrible mistake based on false inklings that were just an effect of an underdeveloped cerebral cortex because everyone else seems to have their act more together. You might even know the feeling of your future being in the hands of outsiders whose rubric is how they feel about you.

Short of being thrown in the express checkout for ordination, I hope that the committee might at least have some direction on what they want me to do or work on in the intervening time. To-do lists soothe me. I make

---

* This is the Episcopal equivalent to the Arabic *Inshallah.*
** Bet you didn't know it was a verb.

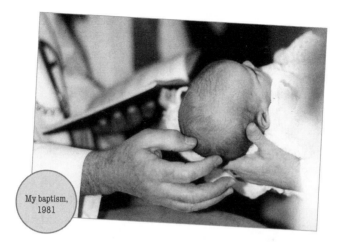

My baptism, 1981

them for days off. Sometimes I even make them after I've already done things—just to be able to cross things off.

I shift in the large, wooden chair. I adopt my most decorous attitude. "Given what you know of my portfolio, what would the committee like to see happen in these coming years?"

The committee rep smiles back, "Well, the committee's main concern for you, Kat, is that you're too goal-oriented, too driven. We'd like to see you grow in 'just being.' Experience what it's like to be in church and not lead worship, really live into your first vows, your baptismal covenant."

This is even more horribly formless than my worst fear. Baptism is what the living do. In the Episcopal tradition it's about living as a person of faith in this life. In fact, when I worked as a hospital chaplain, I wasn't supposed to baptize stillborn babies. I did anyway, though we called it something else. I did it because baptism is what the living do and what the living must go on doing. And if that blond young father—who still kept a wrinkled high school dance picture of him and his wife, all limbs and crinoline, in his wallet—if he wanted a baptism, then I would most assuredly drip water on his daughter's head and dedicate her to God while his wife rocked in the hospital bed holding her stomach, looking away but saying, "Keep going. I'll want to remember this, too…some day."

Hospital cases aside, you'll rarely see a private baptism in the Episcopal Church because the Christian life isn't a private affair, so our initiation rite isn't either. The ceremony is as much about the gathered community promising to try to help raise a child (or adult convert) in the faith as it is about the parents or convert making their own intentions known. Baptism is about living as a person of faith and trying to help others do the same.

But living doesn't follow a specific roadmap, and so the baptismal vow describes the pillars of our faith and general commitments we make to God and one another. It begins with a responsive reading of the ancient Christian creeds between the clergy person celebrating the baptism and everyone else (congregation, baptismal family, the whole gang responding).

Celebrant: Do you believe in God the Father?
People: I believe in God, the Father almighty, creator of heaven and earth.

Celebrant: Do you believe in Jesus Christ, the Son of God?
People: I believe in Jesus Christ, his only Son, our Lord. He was conceived by the power of the Holy Spirit and born of the Virgin Mary. He suffered under Pontius Pilate, was crucified, died, and was buried. He descended to the dead. On the third day he rose again. He ascended into heaven, and is seated at the right hand of the Father. He will come again to judge the living and the dead.

Celebrant: Do you believe in God the Holy Spirit?
People: I believe in the Holy Spirit, the holy catholic Church, the communion of saints, the forgiveness of sins, the resurrection of the body, and the life everlasting.

Then the covenant moves into how we commit to live out our faith.

Celebrant: Will you continue in the apostles' teaching and fellowship, in the breaking of bread, and in the prayers?
People: I will, with God's help.

Celebrant: Will you persevere in resisting evil, and, whenever you fall into sin, repent and return to the Lord?
People: I will, with God's help.

Celebrant: Will you proclaim by word and example the Good News of God in Christ?
People: I will, with God's help.

Celebrant: Will you seek and serve Christ in all persons, loving your neighbor as yourself?
People: I will, with God's help.

Celebrant: Will you strive for justice and peace among all people, and
             respect the dignity of every human being?
People: I will, with God's help.[1]

It's elegant and comprehensive, and yet challenging; individual and yet
communal. Love it. I'm sold.

But I need something to *do* for three years. The woman's suggestion
that I take time to really live into my baptismal covenant was about as
helpful and practical as sitting through a performance art brainstorming
session on the color yellow: "We'd really like to think through what it's like
to be *yellow*. How does yellow sound? What *is* yellow? What would it be
like to embody yellow? Yellow is yolk. Yolk is yellow."

Lord almighty.

Plus, I doubt my own resolve. The Amish send their young adults out
into the world for two years in what is known "rumspringa" to experience
life outside the community before they make a commitment to the Amish
way of life. What if, after my Vegas bender, I decided I didn't want to work
in the church? Then where would I be? Seriously in debt for a professional
degree I wasn't using.

I leave the meeting furious and frightened.

The next weekend I fly to San Francisco for a college friend's weddings.
I relay my tale of whine to other friends out there, over coffee. Outside. *In
January.* "Well," one shrugs in the way that Californians shrug with an air
of *It can't be that bad if you're sitting outside in January*, "You could move
here. The tech industry has shielded the economy a bit, and there's rental
stock, and food is cheap."

Shazam. I can move there. A plan begins to take shape. I interview all
of the clergy I respect to ask them what aspect of ministry they find most
difficult or what they'd do if they had a couple years to prepare. Without
fail, they say, "Finances"—fundraising, stewardship, budgeting, the works
(and fundraising isn't all that different from the work I'd done before seminary as a federal lobbyist).

Well, almost without fail. The woman assigned by the bishop's office
to be my mentor is a priest in an affluent community in southern Connecticut. Her church has recently gone through a horrible personnel issue
involving a music director with child porn found on his church-issued
computer. (See note on extensive background checks I must undergo every
time I apply for a new job within the church.) Suffice it to say that this
woman and her church had been through the wringer when the diocese
assigned her as my mentor.

She answers my inquiry by staring off into space and then slowly responds, "See movies. Take vacations. Enjoy your weekends. Go out every Saturday night if you can. Get together with friends. I don't remember the last time I did that. Once this thing goes on," she taps her clerical collar, "it's all..." Her voice drifts off.

If I were more of an Evangelical, I'd smile and say that one friend finding me a fundraising job at her nonprofit and another friend needing a subletter was a total God thing. But I'm not an Evangelical. So I'll say the same thing but a little differently, which is what usually happens between Evangelicals and Episcopalians. I'll say instead that, for some reason, God was bringing me out to a place where I didn't have a solid sense of identity and community because I needed to fall apart a little bit and grow up a little bit. I needed to scream into the fog that rolls off the Pacific. *What am I if not accomplished? What if I leave Christianity? What if no place ever feels like home? What if I always feel alone?*

You know what happens. This is, after all, a good American coming of age story about a woman on the verge. The year was 2009, when the economy was in shambles but gas prices were still cheap. I was moving to California, where the best-laid plans would fall apart. Hilarity would ensue. The foreshadowing from the introduction comes true. I learn to live out my baptismal covenant.

But this is also an all-American youngish adult love story. It will end with a prom scene of sorts. In college and seminary I fell in love with theology, literally the study of God. Theology tries to break down what we can know and discover about God into a series of questions in order to explore the fullness of God. The discipline isn't without its detractors. Many think that to try to say or codify anything about God is heresy or egotism. No theologian, though, thinks that she will capture or codify God in her proofs. Rather, the goal is to ask more and more questions to come to know and love God more.

During seminary, mine was a May/December romance between me and a bunch of dead white guys. They asked the questions I had long skirted around, but hadn't had the context or language to ask. With them, questions of the relationship between God and life, death, good, evil, eternity, and now were all on the table, a table strewn with highlighters in the wee hours of the morning.

But after graduation, after I stopped gorging on the words of theology like a goose being fattened for *foie gras*, I had to begin to live theologically, integrating the questions I had come to love into the daily rhythm of bills and traffic and coworkers and kids on the playground and pouring maybe too-old creamer into the coffee. An infatuation becomes a lived reality. Each chapter of this book considers a different doctrine of Christian theology to tell a piece of that maturing love story.

I include my love story by way of invitation. I hope that you too have the opportunity to consider and explore these old, crusty questions that have a way of keeping faith new and relevant.

But first I needed to stop in Chicago to rest my beater of a car, kiss my grandmother, and pick up my sister.

Discussion Questions:

- What does baptism mean to you?
- What is the role of baptism in your community?
- Have you had an experience in which it felt like other people were determining your future?
- Have you had an experience of an unwelcome delay?

1

My Grandmother in Black and White

Choice

I stop in to touch base with my yiayia* on the cross-country drive because that's what you do in my family. You stop in to pay your respects to the older folks. When I was little and we lived in north Texas, we would drive from Dallas to Chicago each summer, and we would always have to visit Yiayia and her mother, Big Yiayia, in their six-flat. Big Yiayia was a force of nature who commanded attention, usually from a reclining position on the front porch, where she would complain about her ailments in a heavy Greek accent and gesture with two fingers for Yiayia to do her bidding. *Get the bread. Rotate the fan. Bring me the head of John the Baptist on a platter.*

I had to kiss Big Yiayia on the cheek even when she didn't have her teeth in and black curly hairs sprouted on her chin. While my parents talked to Big Yiayia on the porch, Yiayia would let me keep whichever nail polish I liked best from the basket she kept on the bathroom floor. Old apartments—the combined smells of wood, carpet, radiators, lead paint, and cooking oil—always smell to me like Yiayia's apartment, even my current flat. Sometimes when I pad into the bathroom between waking and sleeping, my foot instinctively moves out to kick the basket of nail polish next to the toilet.

I also stop in because I have Yiayia's car, which she asks after, and I'm not convinced that it will make it to back to Chicago again. I was

---

* "Grandmother" in Greek.

9

Me and
my yiayia

scheduled to begin seminary right around the time Yiayia began to ram her
sensible sedan into large, immobile objects at low speeds. My father and
his brothers agreed that my driving the car out of state would be a good
thing, especially when she began calling local mechanics to say that her car
wouldn't start and could they send someone to look at it. The something
wrong was that her sons had disconnected the battery. Senile and sly as a
fox. When the time came to actually sign the title over, she held the pen
the way children hold crayons, in her fist pointing downward.

"Where are you taking my car?" she asked.

My dad stepped in. "She's going back to school. For philosophy." We
had agreed not to tell Yiayia that I was going to seminary. It was bad
enough that my parents hadn't raised me "in the church," meaning the
Greek Orthodox Church. Instead, my Irish Catholic mother and Greek
Orthodox father had raised us in Protestant churches as a happy medium.
That I was going to become ordained a Protestant minister could resurrect
Yiayia's memories of when my dad married outside the fold. Yiayia was so
upset at their mixed marriage that she refused to walk down the aisle at
either of my parents' wedding ceremonies. Big Yiayia had watched from
her perch and mused casually that if my father had been raised properly,
he never would have married outside.

As Yiayia signed the title over to me in shaky script, she said to me,
"You're just going to keep it running until I'm ready to drive again. I just
need to get better glasses, but it can take a while to find a good pair." So
far it's taken three years to find that pair of glasses.

I visit in small part because I'm preparing to be ordained clergy, and part of what we do is visit the sick and elderly and homebound. I've become something of a pro at listening to stories of sciatica.

But I also come because she is the only living member of my female ancestor mythology. Somewhere in my youth I started this elaborate imagination project of creating a pantheon of my foremothers based on the bits of information I knew about them—and a great deal of whimsy. All would have been grand in another time and place. They were thwarted by their circumstances of poverty and misogyny.

In my version of Yiayia's story, she would have turned her love of literature into work as a professor if finances hadn't required that she work in the family diner after school instead of studying. Big Yiayia forbade her from going to college and instead married her off to my affable grandfather at eighteen. But she lived out her independence in other ways. She took a job as a sales clerk in the men's department at Marshall Field's, and when the evil old boys' network refused to share their retail clients, she built up a cadre of loyal customers who the old boys didn't want: men who liked men. Yiayia's customers asked for her by name and bought many, many fine suits.

We're quite alike, Yiayia and I. We both love books. We both befriended nonstraight people before it was mainstream. Plus, we look alike, from the neck down—or at least we would if she hadn't had four sons by the time she was thirty, and a traumatic brain injury that took away her mobility and her sense of being full when eating. My mother's fair, straight haired, Northern European gene pool had nothing on my dad's Mediterranean DNA strengthened by years in the sun and democratic debates.

But, I also come over because I love my grandmother. It is a mole sauce love—comfortable and familiar and made up of complexities and time.

Yiayia is something of a sandcastle today, beige and mounded up in her recliner. The fact that she's there in the chair with an industrial nylon woven belt always around her middle means that she and her caregiver have already been up for many hours, making the long journey from the bed to the bathroom to the kitchen table to the chair. If her caregiver can pull at just the perfect resistance, and Yiayia can move her feet even a little bit, then the gravitational force of Yiayia-on-the-verge-of-a-faceplant moves the duo forward…provided there's no bump in the carpet. More and more, though, Yiayia's legs just completely give out. As soon as they get her up to standing, her legs crumble; so they use the belt to get her into a wheelchair.

She is watching *The View*. That's good. For many years she watched soaps and could tell you the plotlines of who was having an affair with whom. But then for a while all she wanted was old cartoons. She'd laugh every time a bomb went off in Tom's face as Jerry scampered into a mouse hole. "He got away again!" she'd chortle. Each time.

The View seems like progress. If she were here, I would kiss Barbara Walters and not mention at all that she's starting to look a little windswept.

Yiayia's cheek remains indented where my lips apply pressure in kissing her hello. "Hi Yiayia. It's Kathryn your granddaughter. It's good to see you."

"It's good to see you too." She takes fifteen seconds to say this phrase, which is approximately seven times as long as it would take me to say it. Every word rumbles out in a guttural tone between long pauses. She may or may not reach the end of a phrase before becoming too tired or distracted to finish.

All thoughts and stimuli seem to have equal value to Yiayia. A person talking, a mosquito buzzing, and the garbage truck rumbling outside are equally compelling. She has no separation between foreground and background.

"You say 'your granddaughter' like I don't know who you are," she continues. She's been known to receive a kiss from one of the granddaughters and ask accusingly, "Who are you?" So I introduce myself every time we talk.

I ask if I can turn the TV off so that we can concentrate on talking. She considers my request. Then, finally, "Yes." I reach for the remote before she can change her mind. What were they talking about on *The View*? She says she doesn't know.

Sometimes Yiayia can answer questions, but sometimes I have to monologue. If I happen upon the file of her history that's open at that moment, she'll respond, but it's a crapshoot. I begin by telling her that my youngest sister Margo and I are going to drive cross-country in Yiayia's old car. Margo is seventeen. Can she believe that? That Margo is seventeen?

"No?" She turns to me. I nod. She smiles. That's the right answer. When someone asks a question that ends, *Can you believe it?* the right answer is no.

"Do you remember when Margo was born?"

"Oh, yes. Your father called me, and he said, 'Ma, I have something to tell you. Gayle is having a baby.'" She *does* know who I am. She knows that my father is Chris, married to Gayle, and that my sister is Margo.

"And what did you think?"

"Fine, what did I care? They can have a baby if they want. He called from Hong Kong, you know." *Yes, I do know. I lived with them. I was ten.* "He came back for my surgery. From Japan." *From Hong Kong. You just said it. You know this.*

"That was nice, huh?" I ask.

"Yes. He's a nice boy. He was so nervous about me being sick. They all were."

"Were you nervous?"

She shrugs.

"Do you remember when they told you that you had cancer?" I continue. I don't mean to be imprudent. I'm just curious. I was young when it happened, and no one ever talks about it. There's no one else in the room today, no baby cousin doing somersaults on the carpet or an uncle flipping through her bills to make sure everything is paid.

"Yes."

Very, very long pause. I wait before continuing. Is she done? She's done. "What did you think?"

"I was having these headaches, and so I was saving up to buy some nice down pillows. I was waiting for them to go on sale at Field's. Then I'd use my store discount, but not if they were already sold. Then I couldn't buy them. I was saving up in case I couldn't get them on sale."

"And then they told you you had cancer?" I press.

"Yes."

"And what did you think?"

"I guess I don't need to buy pillows." I chuckle and she just looks at me. Then, she makes the sound of laughter, but her face is blank in confusion. Brain injury is funny that way. Some aspects of decorum, like laughing when others do, remain, but she doesn't know what was funny. She keeps laughing long after I stop.

"Where was the tumor?"

She lifts up what remains of her hair in front. She's balding, and the hair never really grew back around the scar, so she has a comb-over on top. Before menopause and the chemo and the surgery, we had the same, curly hair. My hair went curly in high school, and my mother had no idea how you managed such things. I asked Yiayia what she did when she was younger. She shrugged, "I don't know. Ask your mother." Not helpful—and neither were my cousins who got straight hair. Now, her hair tufts out like Scuttle, the seagull in *The Little Mermaid* after he teases his head feathers with a fork. She's the best indicator I have for how I will age—rounding on the bottom and thinning on the head. She pulls back the hair next to the part on the right hand side of her head and reveals a craggy scar, running somewhat parallel to her part. It's on the right, not the left. All this time I'd been thinking that her scar was on the left, where the comb-over ended, but it's on the right.

It's on the right, so she can't be what I thought, not exactly. I thought I had diagnosed Yiayia as a college freshman. I was that good. In Psych

110 we read about Phineas Gage, the famous construction worker who survived a railroad tie going through his skull. He was the classic example of front left lobe damage. In the pages of the introductory textbook, I thought I had discovered what ailed my grandmother.

Gage was said to have a penchant for the negative after his accident. Yiayia was living in an angry world of the past. She self-defined by every kid in the schoolyard who had called her a name or pulled her hair. Positive memories were entirely slippery, even when we described aloud her sons, her husband, her work at Field's. Only the dull, old hurts offered a toehold to who she was. The worst offender to Yiayia was Big Yiayia, who was dead by then, though you wouldn't know it from the way Yiayia brought her up in constant conversation. We were all subject to an endless recitation of Big Yiayia villain stories, and trying to change the direction of the conversation was futile. Big Yiayia undermined her joy at every turn. Once, I asked if Yiayia remembered anything about the days her sons were born. She shrugged and answered that Big Yiayia said she wasn't a very good mother.

Yiayia's brain refused to let her stay in the present. She couldn't hold onto her siblings or children or grandchildren. It wasn't that she forgot our names or how we fit together, but more that we weren't very interesting to her. Big Yiayia and the pain therein had too strong a hold. If I told her about something going on in my life, she'd remark, "Oh, that's nice, Honey," even if it wasn't something nice, and then her face would go sort of blank for a moment until it settled in a scowl, some familiar painful memory again at the forefront of her mind and face.

Those years of Yiayia's life are one of my versions of hell. She couldn't weigh her memories against one another or alongside her present reality or accomplishments. She couldn't see her life in all its complexity of good and bad, only the unpleasant past on endless replay. It was a loop of one sorrow to the next, something yet more painful behind every door. Neither present reality nor future possibilities had any bearing.

Brain injury took away her ability to frame her life as anything other than tragedy, and it took away her ability to ask or answer the question, "Who are you?" So, in some ways, brain injury removed her ability to form relationships, because that's what an active relationship is, asking again and again in different ways and tumbled tenses, "Who are you?" We ask it of one another and of ourselves and of God and of God about ourselves—*Who are you? Who am I? Who are you in light of your past? Who are you now?*

These questions are what bring us back to one another time after time, to live into the mystery of life together. It's never decided once and for all.

Yiayia's still not able to stay present or to hold onto much new information about another person, but something has shifted in her brain so that other memories are surfacing. There are other characters and nuances in her past I've never heard before. Then again, I'm not sure that I've ever tried to ask her, just the two of us talking, who she is and was. I answered it for her in my imagination, but my answers weren't accurate. She's not Phineas Gage, and she's not a twentieth-century feminist comic book heroine. She's herself.

"How big was the tumor?" I ask her, to keep the conversation going.

"The size of a lemon, they said, before the surgery. And then they said an orange or a grapefruit once they opened it up." She lets her hair flop down. "Sometimes oranges and grapefruits can be the same size, you know."

My parents had used citrus descriptors when they told me Yiayia had a tumor—the size of an orange, and the surgeons had to be very careful. I pictured an osage orange, the inedible, lumpy, yellow-green fruit with a citrus smell that fell along the bike path when we lived in north Texas. The masses have a tough skin that looks, well, rather brainlike, surrounding white, sticky, oozing sap. I figured that the tumor would also leak if punctured. That's why the surgery was so delicate.

"Did the headaches go away then after the surgery?"

"Yes…no… My head hurt different because they had to break it." Long pause. Now she's really done. The file for 1991–1992 is empty or stalled.

"Yiayia, do you remember what it was like to go to your father's restaurant after school?"

"I used to know what kind of people would order what cigarettes."

"Who would order what?" I ask.

"Oh, well, you know young women would order one thing and old men another." Silence. I don't know if the file for 1941 is done.

"Margo and I are leaving from here and driving all the way to California. We downloaded her summer reading list so that we can listen to it on books on tape while we go. Did you have summer reading lists when you went to high school?"

"Oak Park River Forest is a good high school. That's why I stayed in Oak Park for the boys to go there. It was a good high school." This is typical, that she'll defensively answer a different question than one that was asked.

"It still is a good school. Did you ever think about moving?" She scrunches up her face and shakes her head. She stops shaking to stare at the TV, perhaps longingly.

"Do you remember what you read in high school?" She shrugs, face still scrunched. "Did you ever read *Huck Finn* in school?"

"We were supposed to, but I…I read…I got the… You know what I mean."

"*Cliff's Notes*?"

"No!" She shoots back.

"Okay, like an easier version?"

"Yes. Yes. At the library, the ones where it was easier to get the story."

"Were they yellow and black?"

"Maybe?"

"Maybe they weren't."

"Maybe they weren't?" She asks back.

"Maybe the easier version wasn't yellow and black. That's what they looked like when I was in high school, but maybe it was different for you."

"No it was the same as you. Yellow and black. The same. Just like you."* She nods as if to end the discussion.

"Did you like English class?" I change the topic.

"More than algebra. I failed algebra."

She had failed algebra. Perhaps it wasn't all Big Yiayia that kept her from college. The plot thickens. It wasn't all outside forces and circumstance that thwarted her becoming a literature professor.

She continues, "Once I saw my algebra teacher Mr. Reardon here in the neighborhood. He was just walking, and he saw me. I think he was embarrassed to have to see me living nearby, and so he says to me, 'I'm sorry I failed you.' And I said, 'It's okay.'"

"Was it okay?"

"Yes. It was. The teacher would call you to the board to do the problems on the board. The chalkboard. And he'd say Good job, Sam. Oh, right, Ralph. He'd go down the row. I sat far back. Unless we sat by names. I didn't want him to call on me."

"So you didn't raise your hand?"

"No! But he'd just call on you, and you'd have to walk up there and write out the problem. And I could write out the problem, and if it was one that looked just like the example, then I could do it, but not if they changed it."

That's how *I* passed physics and calculus: memorizing the question formats and then what the answers looked like at each step. I never

---

* *Cliff's Notes*, it turns out, debuted in 1958, approximately fifteen years after my grandmother finished high school. It's likely that Yiayia had an illustrated or junior edition of *Huck Finn*.

understood the underlying concepts so that I could apply them together or in any meaningful way.

Silence. Then the file clicks in again. "Everyone would sit down, and I'd be the only one standing there. I'd hold the chalk and look at the board, and everyone in the whole class would be looking at my backside. And I just stood there, not moving until the teacher would say, 'Can you finish it, Sophia?' And I'd say no. And then he'd say, 'Someone go up there and help her.' And I would sit down."

"Were there some classes where you did know the answers?"

"No." Silence. "Well, myths. Because we're Greek, you know," as if this is self-explanatory. "And when the teacher asked who is so-and-so, I raised my hand, and she said 'Yes, Sophia?' And I told her who he was. And then on the next one, too. And she said, 'How do you know that?' And I said my mother taught me."

"She was a good teacher, huh?"

"For that. She taught me the myths when she told me stories about Greece."

Family lore holds that when Yiayia traveled with Big Yiayia back to her little mountain village in Greece one time, Yiayia noticed things in passing that looked exactly like hers—clothing or jewelry or shoes. At first, she thought that she was projecting familiar things the way that you can when traveling—seeing familiar faces only to realize up close that they're strangers. But after the second or third time, she confronted her mother about the fact that all of the village girls were wearing Yiayia's own jewelry and clothes and shoes that had mysteriously gone missing from her closet. Big Yiayia waved her hand, "You didn't even know it was gone. You don't even miss it in America."

"Was algebra the only class you failed?" I ask.

She laughs, and shakes her head no. Then she looks at me sadly, "I never thought that I'd be telling my granddaughter what classes I failed."

I wish, right then, that she didn't know who I was, that the file for who she was talking to had slammed shut in the same instance that her high school memory opened or that I hadn't pried open the high school memory. Her failed classes were hers to keep private and buried. I want, for her sake, to go back thirty seconds, back to the power relationship of the grandmother who took her granddaughter to buy a "first day of school" dress at Marshall Field's that was far too fancy and too expensive for school. It wasn't even on sale. It was full price and navy blue with a white pattern and a name brand my mother never caved to. *Let's go back to there, Yiayia, not here, where I've probed and exposed a scar you find indecent.*

Or let's just go back to companionable silence. We can do that. I can do that. We can be quiet together, and then I won't have flipped over this memory and be holding it, ogling, like kicking over a garden rock whose underside teems with worms and mushrooms and moss all meant for the dark; not because I think that there's anything wrong with the algebra failure but because you do, and even now, even with who you have become, you are still my grandmother, and I love you as that. Or at least I want to.

"I haven't been in high school in a long time. I promise not to use you as an excuse if I ever fail a class."

She pauses and then changes files, "Do you like driving my car?"

"I do." She looks away from me and won't say anything.

I babble nervously, "Thank you for letting me drive it. It's wonderful. I've driven the car every week to jobs and conferences for graduate school all over Connecticut and New York and Massachusetts. Your car has been to Vermont! I couldn't have done any of that if you hadn't let me use your car. Thank you so much."

She doesn't answer.

"Do you miss having your car?"

She turns back to face me, "I see all of these commercials every day on the TV for cars, and I just think…"

File stall. I am about to fill in when the doorbell rings, and my aunt arrives. The conversation is over.

She is so much more complex than I made her out to be. She is now confined to *The View* as her window to the world, but remembers some measure of being able to get up and go when she wanted to in that beater of a sedan. She remembers giving it away. She was mortified in algebra.

She answers the question "Who are you?" differently now than she could have a few years ago in the angry era. But then, wouldn't we all? Isn't self-definition the project always under construction, as our circumstances and experiences change us?

The question "who are you" is living and critical to my relationship with God and others and myself. That I think of the question in the present tense puts me at odds in some ways with two historically significant (and largely Protestant) Christian tenets: double predestination and free will.

Double predestination (at the risk of gross over-simplification) says that from the beginning of time God decided that some folks would be saved and others would not. No matter what, a person's fate was sealed from the beginning of time, from before she was born, and that person couldn't do anything about it. Life on earth was something of a mirage. People might think they had control over what they did and believed, but really God had chosen who would go to heaven and who would go to hell before anyone's birth.*

Northern European Reform theologian John Calvin is credited** with bringing double predestination to the forefront of theology. He explained the concept of double predestination when he wrote, "For all are not created in equal condition; but eternal life is foreordained for some and eternal damnation for others. Therefore, as any person has been directed to one or the other of these ends, we speak of him or her as predestined to life or death."[2] Calvin concedes that the concept raises "some major and difficult questions."

You don't say. Like maybe that some of us are predestined to eternal death and suffering before we are even born, no matter what we do and become in our lives? Or, how could a good and loving God create a baby predestined for eternal death and suffering? Or, why create a beautiful humanity in a fascinating world that's just a *Truman Show* where a tragic script has already been written out?

A second, even more popular tenet in Christian history is free will, or rather, "free-ish will." "Free will" in broad terms assumes that a person is free to chose and make her relationship with God and others over time and throughout time. There's no binding contract. But in the (mostly) Evangelical Protestant construct, "free will," connotes a situation in which a person is free to choose Christ (usually through baptism or some other conversion experience), but that choice is singular and permanent and indelible and will be acknowledged at a future judgment day. Whatever happened in one's life before the choice for Christ and whatever happens after is washed away by the decision of that moment of choosing Christ. A person is sealed in the courts of heaven. Though a person is expected to live in holiness, the proverbial deed has been signed. Hence, I think of it as "free-ish will" because there are significant limitations on the freedom of the will.

I love the reassurance in free-ish will that nothing a person can do will separate her from the love of God, but not the idea that all of what matters rests on one choice at one point in time. We live in contant movement and countless decisions. Some decisions have greater impact than others, but all of them shape our lives with God and one another in this world.

---

* Not to be confused with Single Predestination in which God deems all of humanity good and saved no matter what.

** Oh, I know Theodore Beza and others drove home double-predestination, and it really started with Augustine who waffled on it, but we both know that Calvin gets the credit historically. And it's a great quote.

I can accept that both double predestination and free-ish will assume that we are moving towards some end point. In Chapter 13 I go into great detail about how maybe we're all moving to some creative, wonderful, yet uknown end in which we will be known and judged before God and one another. What I balk at in both doctrines is the idea that our present and ongoing choices and lives don't matter. Both double predestination and free-ish will force our experience of life on earth into a situation in which who we are and most of what we do are irrelevant. In double predestination, God has already definitively decided who is damned. In free-ish will a person decides once to choose God or not, and that's that. If you make the right choice, all before and after is forgiven. If you never make the choice, sucks to be you.

If my relationship with God is a continual one throughout my life, as I hope it is, then who I am and what choices I make and how I frame my history are always in the present tense. This is my real life. I recreate my who-ness with God right now...and now...and even now. I will continue to do so even as I move towards a final, fascinating end.

• • •

A few weeks after our visit, I call Yiayia after driving her car over the Golden Gate Bridge. "Hi, Yiayia. It's Kathryn you granddaughter." Nothing. "I wanted to tell you that I drove you car all the way from Chicago to California, and I just drove over the Golden Gate Bridge."

"Who is this?"

"It's Kathryn. Your granddaughter."

"Why are you calling me? This is my home phone number."

"Yiayia, it's Kathryn. I came to visit a few weeks ago and we talked for a long time. Do you remember that?"

"Who? Yes?"

"Well, I just wanted you to know that I got out to California okay."

"Oh." A laugh track rumbles behind her.

"Yiayia, should I let you go?"

"Go where?"

"I mean, is this not a good time to talk? Should I let you go back to what you were doing before I called?"

"Yes. I...think...I think you should let me go."

"Okay. I love you, Yiayia."

"I love you too. Bye." The words come out at normal speed and coherence. Something ingrained still tells her voice how the words fit together as a phrase. The phone beeps in different tones into my ear as she hits several different buttons before her fingers find "off."

Discussion Questions:

- What, if any, has been your experience with someone whose personality changed because of illness or injury? Did it change who they were?
- How much choice do you think that you have in terms of your present? Your future?
- What do you think about the idea that God has already determined a destiny for people?
- The author argues that the primary question we ask of ourselves, one another, and God is "Who are you?" Do you agree? Why or why not?

2

Time Warp Nebraska
Logical Causality

My goal in road tripping west is to get myself and my stuff to California as cheaply and quickly as possible to get on with life already. My sister Margo's objective is to be able to say that she's been to the beaches of California. I try to warn her that we're going to northern California, not southern—less bikini and more bathing optional (hippies, computer programmers). But Margie is pretty convinced that all California beaches have serious high school lunchroom cache.

By the time we reach Nebraska, we've run out of words. Back when I left for college in 1999, Margo was entering first grade. I haven't been home for more than a summer in the ten years since. We laugh and chat all through Illinois and Missouri. When the radio or life offers nothing to talk about there is always the horizon. Crop dusters hover over fields to kill some species so that others thrive. Flatbed trucks extending a full city block pass us carrying what look like naked, white airplane bodies—but are, in fact, wind turbine blades. And there is an endless array of swooping birds of prey. Margo has a serious and abiding fear of birds. She refers to all of them as "flying carnivores," so when conversation drags, I take great delight in pointing out hawks and vultures, just to get her to shudder. But all of our conversations are wrung out after a couple days.

I look over to the passenger's seat in hopes that Margo has nodded off so that I can listen to National Public Radio, always my default and never hers. She prefers Christian rock, which really is available everywhere. NPR isn't. It's really more SRPR (Selective Regional Public Radio). It's mid-morning so I might still be able to catch the morning news recap.

Me and Margo, looking very surprised, 1992

Margo's face is contorted. Her feet push against the glove box. With all of her high school summer reading lists in books on tape in the foot well there isn't much room to stretch out, but this is different. Her eyes fly open. "We have to stop," she says.

"Are you going to be sick?"

"I see an aura."

Margo started having migraines in middle school. She tries not to get too tired or dehydrated and to anticipate hormonal changes, but sometimes they just sneak up. The only thing to do when they come is to get drugs into her system as quickly as possible and get her into a dark, cold room to ride out the worst of it.

We've just passed a billboard for a Best Western in Ogallala, an upcoming town, and I ask Margo to find the hotel in the AAA turn-by-turn book and call them on my phone. "I can't see the numbers in the book," she answers, and then sucks air through her front teeth.

I hold the steering wheel with one hand and the tour book with the other, reading the phone number aloud and repeating it again and again until I can flip open and dial my phone. We're lucky, the receptionist says, a whole band of truckers just left.

Well that sure is lucky.

By the time I pull into a parking spot near our room, Margo has gone still except for her eyes twitching under her eyelids. I press the room key into her hand and promise to follow with the bags. She shakes her head. "I won't be able to get the key in the door."

She is kneeling at the toilet before I can even turn on a light. Then she falls into a spent sleep with a washcloth over her face.

And then at Lake McConaughy, 2009. Margo changed appreciably in seventeen years.

The day is lost, and maybe more than that. If it is the heat or the rhythm of the billboards or something about the road trip itself that brought on the migraine, then she can't keep driving. We just don't know what caused it. I turn on my computer—facing the wall so that she won't see any flickering—and look up return flight options from each of the cities we have planned to stop in: Laramie and Salt Lake City and Reno. We have to make it to Salt Lake City, at least, to get her home by air.

Migraines leave Margo's brain foggy and her limbs weak, like she's been invaded by a summer storm. For the rest of the day we'll stay away from heat and flickering lights (definitely no 3-D movies). An Internet aerial map of the town shows a huge body of water nearby. The state park website for the lake boasts in Midwestern modesty:

> To most Nebraskans and residents of neighboring states, McConaughy is known as a place for outdoor good times. Its waters and white sand beaches provide the setting for many different kinds of outdoor recreation. Obviously such a fine piece of water offers excellent fishing and boating. But, Big Mac has become a favorite with campers…and other outdoor fun seekers.

How could we pass up "such a fine piece of water"?

Margo awakes midday. We pilfer towels from the motel and sandwiches from a deli in town and explore Big Mac. Deeper and deeper into the prairie we drive, until it feels as if we are in the middle of an ocean of grass without a shore. A windmill on top of a small mound rises like a lighthouse on the horizon. Just beyond the windmill the road turns sharply to parallel a widening river. Then, without warning, the road turns again and deposits us beside a ranger station.

The park ranger apologizes for having to charge us an entry fee (less than half the cost of one of our deli sandwiches), and we park our small sedan among a collection of RVs. Knee-high grasses poke out of sandy soil into our sandals. The ground softens into sand, and the horizon begins to shimmer. At 35,700 surface acres, Big Mac looks nearly as large as the shore of Lake Michigan, where we spent our family vacations growing up. Margo kicks off her flip-flops to walk straight into the water. She giggles as minnows scatter around her, and holds the grocery bag of sandwiches above her head as if the minnows might leap up and make off with our lunch. We wade and sit and read and splash all afternoon. Mud skimmers cautiously approach when we stay still enough. Margo seems to be back to herself. "This is so great," she sighs.

A travel website gives modest endorsement to an old-timey musical theater review down the block from our motel. So we spend the evening watching the best of Ogallala's high school performers stage an old Western, complete with a pistol standoff in the parking lot. A hipster documentary filmmaker who is recording himself going cross country on a donkey is loving the kitsch. But the script for the Western is so long and labored that even the hipster's donkey, tied to a prop hitching post, seems relieved at the last pistol shot.

We are behind schedule, one day further from California, and will have to go slower still to create the most headache-free conditions. But God often messes with my sense of time. I never would have planned to stop in Ogallala, but it is pretty great. Heck, I didn't want to be moving to California to begin with. I wanted to be a priest somewhere in the Northeast, but there I was.

My aunt told me a story once about how she was paying bills in her kitchen in Chicago just before Christmas one year. Her kids were playing in the next room, making sounds of car crashes, buildings burning, and all matter of destruction turning loose. Then a kid yelled, "Use your super powers, baby Jesus!" One of my cousins had incorporated the plastic nativity set characters with the usual action figures. Jesus saved the day—cape, crucifix, and all.

That's something of how Christians tend to interpret history, as if Jesus came into the world as the ultimate roll of duct tape to patch up God's creation that had completely gone off the rails. We read the stories of Hebrew Scriptures, starting with Eden in which humanity is good—as God intended—and then woefully human: full of family strife and war and jealousy and political coups. Then, in the New Testament, Jesus enters, and he takes care of everything. *Ta-dah!*

We repeat this linear history each week in the Episcopal Churches where I worship—Old Testament/Hebrew Scriptures depravity followed by New Testament solution. Telling the history of God's creation of the world and its people, and then the salvation of the world through Jesus, is part of our Eucharist* text. Our instructions for leading the Eucharist are: "The Celebrant gives thanks to God the Father for his work in creation and his revelation of himself to his people... The Celebrant now praises God for the salvation of the world through Jesus Christ our Lord."

The suggested scripts for this service present the stories of creation and salvation as a history in which God created the world and humanity as good. Then humanity messed up. So God redeems the world in Jesus:

> "From the primal elements you brought forth the human race, and blessed us with memory, reason, and skill. You made us the rulers of creation. But we turned against you, and betrayed your trust... Again and again, you called us to return. Through prophets and sages you revealed your righteous Law. And in the fullness of time you sent your only Son..." [3]

Interpreting history this way (Creation good, Creation spoils, Jesus, End) raises some serious questions:

o   Why would God, all knowing and all-powerful, create a world full of creatures that would go berserk?
o   If Adam and Eve set the ball rolling down a bad path, why wait several thousand years to definitively intervene?
o   Sending your child to clean up your mess is not cool.
o   The Hebrew Scriptures weren't a whole series of mistakes.
o   And Jesus wasn't, according to most standard Christian doctrine, an afterthought. The early church councils** determined (through really ugly arguments sometimes resulting in death, wars, or new countries being formed) that Jesus and the Holy Spirit were everywhere and always *coeternal* with God the Father. The Holy Trinity

---

* *aka* "communion," *aka* the "Lord's supper."
**

COUNCIL	ISSUE	OUTCOME
Nicea: 325 C.E.	Is Christ God? Was he always?	Eternal deity of Christ affirmed.
Costantinople: 381 C.E.	Is Christ human? Was he always?	Eternal humanity of Christ affirmed.
Ephesus: 431 C.E.	*Same as Constantinople*	*Same as Constantinople*
Chalcedon: 451 C.E.	How can Christ be fully God and fully human forever and always?	The two eternal natures of Christ are affirmed.
Constantinople II: 553 C.E.	Are we sure?	Yes, we're sure, and anyone who disagrees is a heretic and an anathema.

of Father, Son, and Holy Spirit was together and present from the very start and always intended to be the Trinity.

So, if Jesus was always coeternal with the Father, we have to look at history a little differently. Instead of applying linear causality—one thing leading to another to another—it's more helpful, I think, to use "logical causality." According to logical causality, Christ was always present. God created the world with the overt intention of a God-man who would alter our understanding of past and future. That how a theologian like twentieth century Protestant Karl Barth can say that Jesus was "born in time" to Mary and also "the very same who in eternity is born of the Father."[4] God's presence in the world in human form and spirit form was the plan of the Holy Trinity, so God created the world. God's plan was always revelation, here in the world, in human form. It's as if A and B take place just so that C can happen, but C is not the result of A and B.

Logical causality makes sense to us when we know the end goal. My goal is to get to work, so I pack my lunch, grab my keys, get on my bike, and ride south. Here the linear fits into the logical neatly. The concept is harder when the end goal isn't evident from the start. Think of the discovery of penicillin. Linear causality would say that a rather sloppy scientist fails to clean up his workstation before going on vacation. He returns from vacation to discover a strange fungus on some of his cultures and that bacteria didn't grow where the fungus was.

Logical causality would say that penicillin (or more broadly human wellness) was the goal, so a messy scientist was in a lab where he could get away with messiness, and of course he went on vacation because that was the time needed for the fungus to grow, and of course he would realize what was happening because he was, after all, a research scientist working on bacteria.

According to logical causality God created the world for the express purpose of being present in it as Christ and Spirit, and created and each of us so that God could be in relationship with us. Within that world we choose how we play out our stories, but the logical goal for each of us is a relationship with God. Many religions have a variation on this theme: enlightenment/ flourishing/goodness is the goal for each person, and our lives unfold toward that ultimate goal even if it doesn't always feel that way in the linear experience of time.

Our chronologies twist and turn as we engage in our life choices and outside events, but the C's, the revelations, are the point of A and B happening in the first place. We cannot necessarily see the C's in the midst of living them, but only later, when our chronologies have progressed further along. Later on we can look back and see the logic—events in our lives happened so that a revelation with God could take place.

• • •

After Margo and I make our unplanned stop in Ogallala, our drive continues in a straight line west. Wyoming, we decide, is the most beautiful state in the union. Each hundred miles reveals a complete difference in ecosystem: from prairie to foothills to desert. Utah makes us want to be better Americans with healthier lifestyles. It is the place to be if you are from a limited gene pool that has excised acne, and are prone to strapping on a pair of skis or hopping on a mountain bike, just for the good wholesome fun of it.

And Nevada…Nevada is proof positive for conspiracy theorists' worst assessments. There really are aliens and black helicopters and Hoffa's body hidden in a shallow grave surrounded by nuclear testing refuse. It is an alternative reality through which you must pass between fresh-faced Utah and affluent Lake Tahoe, California.

Nevada is seeded with distractions to keep us from asking too many questions. One gas station is staffed by an off-hours showgirl—complete with blue sequins still glued to her fake eyelashes, and a feather headdress lying on the counter next to the cigarettes. Another gas station is guarded by a man with a huge "shiner," spitting brown tobacco slobber into an old Gatorade bottle. His good eye tracks our every move. Both stations' have slot machines inside the *bathrooms*. Less appealing machine levers have never existed.

As lunchtime approaches, we see a sign from God—golden arches of familiarity.

"Dad worked at a McDonalds in high school," Margo recalls.

"Yeah."

"He's a good dad."

"He is. I love him"

"We should call him."

"Yeah."

"Maybe just hear his voice one more time."

I order a Happy Meal to remind myself that God's creatures are still producing a new, hopeful generation that watches Disney movies and plays with plastic figurines. We huddle in a corner booth and dial home.

"Hi Daddy," I begin. "We're in Nevada. We just passed through… through some no man's land. I don't know what it's called."

A voice booms from the opposite side of the restaurant. "The Bonneville Salt Flats. It's called the Bonneville Salt Flats. Nothing can live there." Margo and I sit bolt upright and lock eyes with the speaker, a gangly teenager in a stained T-shirt who stares at us, nodding. The place must have an echo chamber that allows for covert conversation tapping. We are not safe. We stuff our food into the greasy paper bag and make for the car.

It takes what feels like approximately three years to get through the Lake Tahoe region and into the live heat of Sacramento, because I am the world's most timid mountain pass driver, and Yiayia's car does not do uphill well—not while weighed down with two girls and one's worldly possessions. Finally, after dropping our bags at the apartment I'd be living in for the next year, we head for the beach. The GPS directions read simply, "Continue to the Pacific Ocean."

Half Moon Bay is so overcast that the park ranger waives our entrance fee. Wind whips cold fog droplets at every bit of exposed skin. I mummywrap myself an old blanket and lay on the wet sand, my hip throbbing from days of driving. Margo, hoping for a California beach experience, chatters beside me in a swimsuit and flip-flops.

I have just begun to drift off, when Margo shrieks, "That's it! I am out of here." A carnivorous seagull has tried to peck at her toe. That is her one and only California beach experience. She doesn't even bring in up when she talks about our trip. Instead, she talks about Lake Big Mac, and about the creepy kid in Nevada, and about radio battles in which she had to teach her super-dorky older sister a thing or two about contemporary radio.

What if being marooned in Nebraska was the whole point of driving through Missouri and Illinois, or even the point of the whole road trip? Logical causality honors that our stories, our lives, are complicated, as are the narratives in the Hebrew Scriptures. Cain is both the original murderer and the forefather of humanity. Jacob is a greedy two-timing jerk and the father of all nations. The Israelites are God's chosen people and engage in endless tribal wars with the Babylonians and other ancient peoples. Neither their stories nor our stories are linear. We are our best and worst selves. But God is always present and always redeeming, even when we cannot see God at work in real time.

Our lives really are our lives, full of freedom and pain and joy. And we do not live out our days in some neener-neener Nevada Twilight Zone in which we lack control of our lives and time. Rather, God is present—and always intended to be present—with us in the world. We're not always aware of God or of the path that we're on, but God is always there, leading us towards our C's of revelation and relationship.

Eventually Margo heads home to Chicago, but not before a really lovely dinner with friends.

Discussion Questions:

- Have you had an interruption in life that ended up being wonderful? Or even difficult, but valuable in some way?
- The author accepts the concept that Jesus and the Holy Spirit were coeternal with the God the Father—existing from before the world was created. How does this align with your understanding of Christianity?
- Does the framework of logical causality work with your understanding of the Christian story? Why or why not?

3

Bible Says

How We Read

The family friends from Hong Kong invite Margo and me to dinner at their tour-of-homes-beautiful abode. The furniture is black lacquer with gold and red cushions. Framed swords and ceremonial robes purchased during the years we all lived as expatriates hang on the walls. I haven't seen these friends since we all moved back to the states almost twenty years ago, but I understand why my parents wooed them as surrogate family. Both families had been transferred to Asia in the late 1980s for both fathers' jobs with tech companies. Hong Kong, then a British colony, was the gateway to China—a bazillion people who didn't know that what they really, really wanted was a cell phone.

They're tight huggers. I remember this when I slam into the husband's barrel chest, and he's wearing the same cologne he did in Hong Kong. The scent memory takes me back to Thanksgivings we spent together, with a turkey tasting vaguely of seafood because all of the poultry in that region of Southeast Asia were fed a diet of fish scraps. I remember too how the wife would pull me into an embrace at eye level with her cleavage and would whisk baby Margo into her voluminous scarves at church, claiming her prerogative as Margo's Hong Kong godmother.

The wife's hands are in endearing constant motion. Her perennially red finger nails touch my arm, hold my hand, pull out a cutting board, and then pull out a bamboo and lace fan from somewhere in the folds of her black scarf. "Aren't you so hot in here? I'm opening a window. Honey, open a window. Kathryn and I are hot." Without missing a beat the fan disappears again, and she begins to chop zucchini. Margo just watches in sheer overstimulation. She doesn't remember the couple, but they look exactly the same to me: some ambiguous age between fifty and seventy, and all rounded edges—round cheeks and heads and noses and shoulders. She has dark, loose, chin-length waves of hair and dark, rounded nails. He is balder, I suppose, but not appreciably older.

As much as I enjoyed them as a child, I think that I like the couple even more as an adult. My affection isn't just a matter of vestigial loyalty. They are funny and kind and warm and smart. Plus, their forks are heavy in the hand; their wine glasses actually crystal.

"So," initiates the husband, immediately after table grace, "Is the Episcopal Church going to split over the gay issue?"

The lights in the room begin to fade. Spotlights rise over my head and his, but they hover. The moment could go in any direction. "I'm not sure. I'm not really sure that it's actually a question about sexuality so much as about colonialism, about the church in the Southern Hemisphere claiming its own identity against the U.S."

"But the Episcopal Church in the U.S. is pretty liberal, right?"

"Well…"

"Will you marry gays?" he interrupts.

"I'll perform a blessing for two adults who have been through planning and counseling and want to make a Christian commitment." I answer as though reporters might be lurking under the kitchen counters for a sound bite.

"See, that's what I don't get! Now, maybe I'm ignorant here on the Bible. And so I'm asking you because you're the expert, but in the Bible homosexuality is pretty clearly a sin, right?"

"Honey!" The wife's hands are in the air in some version of the international sign for *You're making our dinner guest uncomfortable.* But it's too late. She fades to black. Spotlight on me. Margo is completely under the table, dying a slow and painful death flanked by the two miniature poodles that dart at our feet.

What neither the wife nor my sister seem to appreciate, though, is that I really do like this man, and while I'm not wild about engaging in this conversation right now, it's part of my job as a Christian to read the Bible with others to the extent that I am able. Part of what Christians do is engage the biblical text.

The question my host poses is not a matter of being an expert in terms of quantity of Bible verses or knowing the right biblical scholarship or the right themes. Anyone can search the Bible and find quotes either directly or thematically related to many, many topics. Advice in one verse often differs from another passage. Textile blends? Facial hair? Lust? Killing? The Bible contains different responses depending on the passage you choose.

The complexity arises because the Bible is an anthology. The Old and New Testaments are a collection of folk stories, legislation, poems, songs, and letters written over several hundred years. The texts are holy and contain holy wisdom, but the pieces do not create a unified narrative or linear history. It's as though the *Iliad*, pieces of *Canterbury Tales* and *Beowulf*, the *Magna Carta*, a history of the Tudor monarchy, American frontier folk songs, excerpts of the *Bill of Rights*, and some O. Henry stories were all gathered between two covers. The texts are a compilation that can be read in some sort of conversation with one another, but not as a single A–Z story, nor a forthright users' manual with a topical index.

Reading the Bible with expertise isn't a question of who has access to more biblical scholarship. Rarely do two scholars agree on exact translation, intended audience, and meaning. I did a study a while back on the first chapter of Romans—one of the only passages in Scripture on non-hetero sexuality and the only one to discuss non-hetero behavior by women. One of my favorite commentaries on this passage comes from the fourth-century commentator Ambrosiaster. He writes about Romans 1:26, "Paul tells us that these things came about, that a woman should lust after another woman, because God was angry at the human race because of its idolatry. Those who interpret this differently do not understand the force of the argument."[5] In other words, anyone who disagrees with Ambrosiaster is a fool, which means, presumably, that some disagreed with him. Scholars always disagree. They disagreed in the fourth century, and they disagree now.

Nor is reading the Bible and interpreting it properly a question of who is pulling out the right themes. With some variation in emphasis, many Christians can agree that the Bible is a testament to God's revelation as the Trinity (Father, Son, and Holy Spirit) and God's message of faith, hope, and love for the world.

We use passages from the Bible the same way we use statistics. Sometimes we use them to inform our opinions, but more often than not we use them to reinforce what we've already made up our minds about. We back up into the text. Rather than asking, "What does the Bible say about X?" a more helpful question, I find, is: "What do you hope that the Bible will say about X? Why?"* Then, then we can have a conversation.

If we asked *that* question—which we don't at this dinner—but if we did, I could tell my dinner host about my first kiss. It was staged. Three sections of orange upholstered seating spread out in a fan of the high school auditorium. I played Bella, the mentally off aunt in Neil Simon's *Lost in Yonkers*. Farid played my romantic interest. We were both sixteen.

---

* Or, "What do you hope the Bible will say about X? Y? (*Tee hee.*)

It was romantic, really—surrounded by our classmates in period costumes that smelled of other peoples' sweat and pancake make-up.

We held off on actually kissing as long as possible. In rehearsals we marked the blocking for the kiss, just facing one another and puckering and quickly turning away. Farid's parents had emigrated from Algeria when he was an infant to escape civil war. He had a habit of applying Chapstick, licking his lips, and then kissing the air. When we finally kissed (closed mouth) at the final dress rehearsal my lips came away shiny and wet, as if I had been bumped from behind when about to eat a forkful of chicken. Kissing was perhaps a natural progression after spending nearly every day after school in rehearsal for something or another, every Saturday between October and March at some theater competition, and many school dances straddling him in public. Allow me to explain.

Because I have pictures taken in front of fireplaces of my friends' homes to document each of the dances—groups of braces and satin-clad teenagers—I know that I had various dates, and even went stag to Homecoming one year. But Farid was my dominant and default date. Our signature move on the dance floor was a swing-style partner lift that we'd learned for a show choir *Grease* medley. I would get a labored running start and then jump up onto Farid, interlacing my fingers behind his neck while bracing my forearms against his collar bones. Using the momentum from my running start he'd swing my legs to his left side, then the right side, straight up to gain force for the big move. In the *piece de resistance*, I would swing in to straddle him and then end (ideally) in a stand. Sometimes the move was left, right, straddle, roll-and-try-to-make-it-look-intentional as I got to my feet before the final eight count.

I liked our move. Farid loved our move. We agreed it was a skill that ought not be limited to only a staged Broadway medley in matching sequins. We adapted the sequence for straighter skirts by eliminating the straddle and took our show on the road of many, many high school dances. What makes a good pop song great? A partnered swing routine! At the least provocation Farid would grab my hand, and we'd begin to dance with bigger and bigger gestures and twirls, opening an observer ring around us. Then he'd wink at me, move back a few feet in rhythm to the music and slap his thighs twice. I'd take my running start. Aside from the time I accidentally kicked a girl in the mouth and her braces cut through her lips leaving her bleeding down the front of her dress, our shtick was fun.

None of the theater crowd was exactly surprised when Farid came out of the closet our junior year. We weren't sure how to react, though, when his parents kicked him out. Another theater geek girl and her single mother took Farid in to live with them for the rest of high school. Sometimes

Farid smelled bad because now he had to buy his own deodorant, and in a household of all women, he'd forget to put it on the grocery list. Maybe, I thought, maybe his parents were just being Algerian.

But being Algerian didn't account for what happened the one afternoon Farid asked me to drive him over to his parents' house to pick up some clothes he had left there when moving out. I'd driven Farid home a thousand times before. He didn't have a car and was a complete ride hog, never offering to chip in for gas and never once inviting me in. He'd just jump out at the curb. This time, though, he asked me to come in with him.

As soon as we walked inside, Farid's mother flew into the foyer where we stood.

"Get out! Get out!" she shrieked. "You disgust me. You sleep with men? You take it from them? You are not my son. I'm changing the locks."

"I just need to…"

"You are a sickness. Get out." Then she turned to me, pointed her finger at my chest and began, "And you? Are you like him? Do you go with women? Or do you just take it from men from behind like he does?"

No words came out of my mouth.

"Go to the car," Farid told me quietly.

Shaking, I sat in the front seat of my parents' minivan, and pulled it forward a house length, idling. Arms full of clothes, Farid climbed into the passenger's seat a few minutes later. "I'm sorry for that. I didn't think she'd do it if you were there."

I had never before and have never since witnessed such vile hatred directed at a person, outside the context of a scripted play.

Maybe, I thought, his mother was fitting in with the neighborhood. One of the other guys I went to a dance with had a sister who came out as a lesbian while we were all in high school. He heartily supported his parents in kicking her out of the house. They were all red-headed Catholics who had been in the Chicago area for generations.

Margo goes to the same high school I did, and I am amazed by the off-hand anecdotes she tells of friends of hers who are "bi-curious and totally just experimenting" and teachers who are open about their same-sex partners. When I was there just a decade earlier, "See You at the Pole"—a nationwide day of prayer—was the largest student gathering each year at the school, even though it wasn't school-sanctioned. The communal prayer had a much larger turnout than the Homecoming football game, which is saying a lot for my ultra-spirited school. The girls' bathroom stalls were defaced with Jesus fish symbols and John 3:16. Almost equally palpable was homophobia, and so it was quite the statement when Farid founded the Gay-Straight Alliance and a few of us joined in solidarity.

Soon Farid's world became Gay. Everything was an entrée to discuss sexuality, even math class. *I'll give you an irrational number—it's called a queer teen!* He almost lost his first name the way young physicians do when they introduce themselves as "Doctor." He was Gay, and also his name was Farid.

One afternoon of our senior year, we sat on the floor with our backs against some lockers while we waited for our rehearsal slot. "So, you're a Christian," Farid began.

"Yep," I answered.

"And, I'm gay."

"You're way gay," I corrected.

"Way gay," he agreed and then fell silent, twisting a combination lock above his head. "Do you think I'm going to hell?"

"Nope."

"Because in the Bible…"

And before I could stop myself, I exploded, "Jesus says jack about homosexuality in the Bible." I was just getting warmed up. "Some Christians will say horrible, hateful things to you. I won't. I'm sorry that they will. But I won't. Who you are is not a sin." Then we sat there quietly holding hands until the door of the classroom opened, and we went in to practice.

I spoke before I had the academic and theological underpinning to back up my statements, but my teenage brain spoke the same words I'd say again today. Who he was was funny and created by a loving God. When I read scripture, I find too much biblical evidence for compassion and God's desire for all of God's creation to flourish to condemn Farid.

My resolve was cemented some years later on an otherwise forgettable February day when I received an e-mail informing me that Farid had committed suicide. Farid is unique to me because he was my friend, but he is not unique statistically. In the United States the number one cause of death among queer youth is suicide.

When I read scripture in light of questions about non-hetero sexuality, Farid is my lens. I read the Bible hoping that I will find something that will make him want to live. What would reassure him that he was perfectly created in the image of a loving God? What interpretation would reinforce love of God and love of other people? My dinner host's life and background have led to a very different reading of scripture, one that runs counter to mine, but both are valid, Christian interpretations.

I hate these situations in which I read scripture with people whose lives and vantage points run counter to mine. In some ways, it would be so much easier if there was just one, accurate interpretation of each passage of the Bible, but that would mean reversing the course of history, back to a time before homosexuality was an open social issue.

We'd have to go back before the Civil War. In the eighteenth and nine-teenth centuries, American Christian communities were absolutely ripped apart over Biblical interpretations around the issue of slavery. Both sides had historical and theological merit. Both found passages and scholarship to support their interpretations. Abolitionists made intra-scriptural argu-ments against slavery, finding human dignity and freedom the pervasive theme in scripture. Slave-holding Christians and their supporters argued that slave holding was supported in the Bible. Both were correct.

Then we'd need to go back before broad-based literacy and before the Protestant Reformation, which resulted in the Bible being put into the lan-guages and hands of Christians in churches. We'd need to go back further still to a time when clerics didn't debate the meaning of scripture among themselves.

To find one, single, agreed-upon, valid interpretation of scripture, we'd need to go back to a time that maybe never was and certainly isn't now. As long as people have been reading scripture, they've been struggling to interpret the text for their present situations.

For some Christians, reading the Bible with multiple valid interpre-tations strips the Bible of its authority as Scripture. If the word of God can't tell an accurate history of the world, and be a guide for what should be—everywhere and always—then what good is it? They might say that if the Bible is indeed the word of God, then every word must speak the same message in any translation at any time. Furthermore, they could argue that the Bible is very clear on what's right and what's wrong. Reading the Bible isn't hard at all. What's hard is subsuming your life to its authorita-tive principles.

But we choose what principles have authority, and those choices are hard. What speaks to God's revelation of faith, hope, and love? It's a con-versation that has no end. In this world, we just have ourselves and our rich, complex lives, and the Bible as an open book between us.

I could engage my dinner host in the question of why he wanted the Bible to condemn homosexuality. But I don't. The wife jumps in and says something about it being a generational divide, how their daughter, who's my age and was my childhood friend, sees no problem with being Chris-tian and pro-gay. I nod. Maybe thirty years into the future, I will be the one hosting some young person to dinner, baffled by how she can inter-pret her position on some issue I'm yet to envision in light of scripture. I see Margo's eyes pleading with me not to derail dinner, and I am tired.

Tonight I am just too tired to have a long, hard conversation; too tired to take the bait or raise the banner; too tired to sit together with him, reading the Bible and considering the nature of God as revealed in scripture and in our lives. I hope, in these moments, that my person is enough testimony; that my decision to be a Christian who fully supports gay people and intentionally chooses to be in a denomination that does too suffices as a statement. There are times when I have to trust that there will be more times in the future to talk hard. So I stay seated, blink, and sip my wine.

The dinner continues skittishly, unresolved, for we have opened a conversation and just left it there. But isn't that what we do with people we love? We open hard conversations, and sometimes we have them, and sometimes we walk away from them angry or hurt or confused, and sometimes we just open them and leave them there breathing and oozing to be continued.

At the end of the night, our hosts send Margo and me home with gallon-sized bags of leftovers.

Discussion Questions:

- The author suggests that there can be multiple valid, Christian interpretations of scripture, even if they oppose one another. What do you think?
- Is it fair to open a question about scripture with, "What do you hope the scripture will say?"
- How do debates about scripture make you feel?
- If you found yourself in a situation like the author at dinner, how would you handle it? Have you ever been in a similar situation?

4

Luke, This Is Your Father
The Voice of God

Megan, the girl whose apartment I'll be living in, is an indirect friend and one so nice it makes my teeth hurt. When we pull up to the apartment she's leaving to me, there's a handmade sign on the door reading, "Welcome home, Kat and Margo!!!" There is an enormous salad and pitcher of iced herbal tea on the table, which is exactly what you want after a week of Taco Bell in the Bonneville Salt Flats. She insists that we stay in her bed and carves out a space for herself on the living room floor, among the dozens of boxes of books I have sent ahead of me.

She looks every bit the California girl—with long, blond hair and a straight, shiny smile. That she's smiling is a testament to her grit and modern medicine. Megan was born with a misaligned jaw. The whole time I'd known her, she was like a subject model whose cheek Picasso had caressed on his way out the door. Several medically necessary surgeries, a year of leave from graduate school during which she'd existed on a liquid diet while her head healed into a new normal, and extensive orthodontia later, her smile is earned.

My friendship with Megan was always through someone else, which makes it all the weirder to be taking over her apartment. I think that I must have met her through college activism, maybe at a Students Against Sweatshops rally. She was always just there, quietly off to the side, chiming in on protest songs with intuitive harmonies but never taking the megaphone.

The Students Against Sweatshops were like Amos or Micah, the nice prophets in the Hebrew Scriptures, who used socially acceptable means to call those in power to justice. They talk at people to tell them to turn back from ways of injustice. Sweatshop labor protests involved people sitting outside the president's office in formless clothing, demanding that Yale pull out of investing its endowment funds in countries that permit sweatshop labor. I sat in on the protests because it's activist etiquette to support one another's causes by showing up.

I focused my activist efforts on the U.S. war on drugs. Drug-related felonies—but not rape or murder*—resulted in lifetime ineligibility for federal financial aid for higher education. Once a person had served time for a drug felony, that person couldn't receive any aid to help go back to school and gain the sorts of skills needed to obtain a living wage job. The impact was particularly widespread in communities of color.

Working on the drug war was a way that I could work on race issues, which is not easy to do. Despite the many generations since the Civil War, we still don't know how to really talk about or work on racial equality, at least not from the white side of things. Battling against an obscure provision in the Higher Education Act offered a tangible way to try and be part of the solution.

Yale's drug war activists decided that the best way to address this injustice was to demand that the university commit to covering the financial aid for all students who were admitted to Yale after serving their sentences but who couldn't receive the financial aid they would have received otherwise. It would be a situation of an institution of power speaking out against what we considered to be an unjust law.

Our protests were more like something orchestrated by the prophet Ezekiel, who used public theater tactics to get peoples' attention. At one point, Ezekiel hears God tell him that the only way to warn Jerusalem about the city's imminent destruction is to build a pint-sized model of Jerusalem out of bricks and then surround the brick model city with attack camps. Then, just in case someone passing by was to ignore the brick model city under attack, Ezekiel lies on the ground with his face separated from the brick models by an iron plate. *For 390 days.* And during the whole 390 days he eats only whole grain cakes baked on a fire of human poop. Subtle. But he got some attention with his antics.

Drug war protests had crazy chanting and dramatic staging. Our brainstorm sessions produced ideas involving men on stilts, larger-than-life papier-mâché puppets, and white guys with dreadlocks scaling the Yale president's office building Spiderman-style with construction paper marijuana taped to their backpacks yelling, "I can only do this because I'm white!" Scaling the administration building was only rejected because we

---

* Or pillaging or marauding.

couldn't find night goggles, and it had somehow been determined that the public theater would only really have the desired impact if the grungy guys had night goggles too. Go figure.

After months of demanding a meeting with the administration, we received an invitation to come to the president's office. This was a total surprise. My activism was buoyed by the notion of being involved in modern-day prophecy—of calling people to attend to injustice for the poor and oppressed. *Viva la revolución.* I never thought we'd actually get something.

I walked into the administration building with a coprotester of mine on the appointed meeting day, fully expecting to be in a royal chamber of sorts. But there were no armed guards, just some rather tired-looking secretaries who waved us down the hall. The meeting room lacked silver tea service, and the leather covering on the seats was starting to separate from the frame. Across from my friend and me sat one of the president's advisors and Yale's lobbyist.

My friend and I were very quiet all of a sudden. We were shocked (*shocked!*) to find out that this issue was not a high financial aid priority for other universities, who were all in some sort of lobbying posse together. After all, we were in regular conversation with other schools' drug war activists. The lobbyist asked if we had gone in to see our local Congressional or Senate staff on this. *Umm, no.* Did we know when the relevant law was coming up for reauthorization? *Er, no.* (Did I know what reauthorization was? *Ditto*).

Things changed that day at the conference table. Institutionally they changed because the university agreed to cover the financial aid for anyone whose financial aid was denied because of a drug felony.* Personally, though, I was changed by listening to the lobbyist's questions. I wanted to know what he did in terms of specific steps involved in legislative change, when and how a person did what for the authorization or reauthorization of a bill. Thus began my conversion from activist to policy-wonk lobbyist.

After college, Megan and I both found ourselves carving out lives in Washington, D.C. She lived with a mutual friend in a basement apartment in a changing neighborhood. The window air conditioner units hummed at a monstrous volume and sent rivers of condensation down the walls in a rusty delta, but served to drown out the conversation of the loiterers on the front stoop. The girls tried as best they could to brighten things up with scarves and company. They'd have me over for the vegetarian fare we

---

* This decision likely followed outside research on the odds of ever having to make good on this commitment in the future, since the chances of someone getting out of jail for a drug felony and then accepted to Yale on academic merit were rather slim.

could afford on nonprofit salaries and D.C. rents. When we gathered, we would commiserate over how different post-college was from what we'd imagined.

Somehow I didn't get the memo on how difficult first jobs out of college are. Content-wise they're not impossible, but I missed school. *Had I conducted myself at a "B+" level in that meeting?* I dreamt of working really hard on a paper and then being done with it completely, instead of muddling through long, drawn-out, continual projects. After a lifetime of relatively solitary schoolwork, there were so many people calling and e-mailing and yelling all the time—and so much, it seemed, was at stake. As much as I'd wanted relevant work, this was a little too weighty. If I did my job well there would be money for a homeless shelter in Harlem, but if I didn't… Plus, none of the women at the top of the organizations where I worked had children. I had no role models or vision for how I could have a career in lobbying and also children, or at least children I spent enough time with to know well.

One night of particularly strong freefall, Megan looked across her hand-me-down table to me and said, "Just remember to eat lots of vegetables." Her words stuck with me, because of their sheer absurdity (or so I thought at the time). So I mentioned Megan's comment at my Bible study group. A half dozen of us gathered each week at the apartment of a guy from the Pacific Northwest and his English bride. Catriona, the wife, did not suffer fools. There were many fools to be had—our government, our health insurance system, our lack of puffins on tiny islands, our snack foods that had been so heavily processed that they couldn't harm a molar. She welcomed us into her proper British home each week with a spread of stout tea and grainy biscuits that doubled as laxatives. We'd gather (the nonprofit types, the actress, the aspiring diplomat, the graduate students) to listen to one another's stories, read some scripture, and try to figure out where and how God was appearing in each of our lives.

When I relayed Megan's comment to the gathered crowd who pretended to nibble the edges of hearty biscuits, Catriona said, "Not crazy at all. I was actually going to ask if you were still running enough. I think that God's telling you to stay healthy and wait for further instructions."

The whole room nodded and waited for my response. *Ummm*, well, I guess I wasn't eating as many vegetables or running as much as I ought to. I sort of shrugged, and the conversation moved on to the next person's check in.

Seriously? I was in existential angst (pronounced "ahngst" for pomposity), and the holy wisdom I got back was to eat some broccoli and strap on my Nikes? That's exactly what was happening, according to my Bible study friends. God was telling me to keep myself healthy and to hang in there through the growing and discovery period.

In the Christian tradition, in order to discern between what is wisdom from on high and what is static, a series of questions are considered. These questions follow one another almost seamlessly, so it's helpful to parse out what took place in the exchange I just mentioned. My example sort of loosely follows the Ignatian spirituality*, but it's replicated across various models for revelation in the midst of life.

1. Question yourself. The individual begins by asking him/herself, "Why am I remembering this comment?" We hear thousands of words each day, so we consider in our own minds and hearts why one particular comment is sticking. We may ask God about it in prayer, but it's an internal dialogue.

2. Seek out other Christian listeners for outside perspectives. After posing the question to yourself, approach trusted companions on life's journey and bring the situation to them. Many Christians believe that God's voice is discerned and figured out in community with other people of faith.

There's an oft-told story in seminaries. A young man goes to his pastor/ bishop/priest/elder/metropolitan/choose-your-religious-authority-figure and says, "I have heard God's voice, and I believe that God is telling me to quit my job and become a missionary/enter the priesthood/leave my wife/ learn pantomime." The religious authority figure strokes his beard and responds, "That's funny. I was just talking to God, and he told me no such thing." The young man leaves in despair and goes back to the life he was trying so hard to escape, for he has not in fact heard the word of God. We discern God's voice with one another, never alone.

Christian companions listen to your story with three questions in as they try to help you figure out whether, in fact, you might be hearing a message from God. They begin by asking themselves, "How does the message align with what I know about the person?" Put differently, "How does this situation align with the person I know, created by God?" Catriona knew from having run a few races with me that I needed a certain amount of exercise each day in order to keep believing that the world was a good place, and that I was best off eating a rabbit's farm worth of veggies.

---

* Ignatius Loyola (d. 1556) was a Basque aristocrat who converted to Christianity while convalescing from war wounds. He began a pattern of lifeline spiritual journeying that involved regularly asking questions or "examens" to reflect on ones emotional life to consider where and how God is calling one to be and do in the world. In the general bucket of what is known as Ignatian flavored spirituality now, a person reflects on the examens twice daily on her own, on retreats, with a spiritual coach known as a spiritual director, and with others.

Then the Christian companion considers, "How does this align with what I know about the nature of God as revealed in the Bible?" It's up to the individual to determine her own overarching themes of the Bible, but, as I read it, we get stories of God creating humanity out of love and being present to humanity throughout years of wandering and twisting and turning, always edging us toward flourishing and bringing about justice, even though we try to thwart the effort.

Looking back, I see myself a bit in the story of the Israelites in Exodus, wandering around the desert. I was trying to figure out what to do with life post-college. The Israelites wanted out of the desert after their years of struggle, and instead God gives them nutritious food to sustain them. I wanted out of my early twenties, and instead I was reminded to eat vegetables.

The Christian listener then adds one final question: "How does this situation line up with what I know about God as revealed in the person of Jesus?" In Christ, God reveals that humanity is so precious to God, that nothing we do and nothing done to us can separate us from that love. God desires to be with us in our very messy, cloudy human state. I believe that, in the person of Jesus, God shows us that we are never alone; however, sometimes the way forward isn't clear until we wait with the discomfort. I'm not sure what my listening companions thought.

I was still loved and redeemed, but God was recreating something in me, and I needed to wait. *Awesome*. Thanks.

• • •

We are our next selves now, Megan and I. Post-seminary, I am moving into Megan's apartment in Northern California to take over her rent for a year while she does dissertation research in Russia. I will be riding her bike and sleeping in her bed and cooking with her spices. She has even arranged for me to meet most of her friends, so that I know people in the area.

I can't help but feeling like I am really overstaying my welcome. I tell Megan about my reservations after we send Margo back to Chicago.

Megan asks if I remember having dinner at her apartment in D.C. I retell her the "eat vegetables" bit. Megan doesn't remember saying that at all, though she admits that it does sound like something she'd say. The dinner she was thinking about was when she was debating whether to accept a graduate school offer at Stanford, clear across the country, thousands of miles from family and familiarity. I'd promised her that it would be a grand adventure and that she'd be able to play outside year round for study breaks. I don't remember it. She tells me that our conversation that night in D.C. gave her the courage to take the Stanford offer and that I'd never be subletting from her if I hadn't given her encouragement in the past. Plus, she reminds me, I am paying her rent and keeping her from having to put her stuff in storage or find a new place to live when she returns from Russia. "I'm not that nice," she laughs.

I can see now that in those early years of adulthood, we were trying out different selves and making turns to become the people we would become—people more and less radical than the selves we'd imagined ourselves to be as college activists. We were, as the author of Ephesians writes, "growing one another up." We were collective—if unaware—mouthpieces for God, made all the more unaware because we lived at the edges of each other's lives. The conversations in California are among the longest we've ever had, just the two of us.

Sometimes the voice of God is heard through gentle prophets such as Amos, or zany ones such as Ezekiel, calling their communities to move in different directions. Sometimes the voice of God comes through that of a friend, but sometimes not a close friend; rather, a person we wouldn't otherwise think twice about until she says something that hits us funny.

In all cases, though, the voice is muffled, and together we pick out the gold from the dross to see how the voice aligns with what we know about God and one another. Blaise Pascal writes, "What can be seen on earth points to neither the total absence nor the obvious present of divinity, but to the presence of a hidden God."[6] We seek God out of hiding for one another—story by story, meal by meal.

Discussion Questions:

- Who are the people who help you discern God's voice?
- Have there been times that you've been surprised by what they've said?
- For whom are you a trusted counselor? Do you follow any sort of process in discerning with people?
- Has a friend or acquaintance ever said anything to you that seemed odd or random, but later turned out to be exactly what you needed to hear?

5

Gross

Sanctification

In parts of the ancient world, women were thought to be wet and leaky—prone to uncontrollable and therefore dangerous bodily fluid releases of all sorts. The purity codes of Judaism forbade a woman from entering the Temple during and immediately following menstruation. Her fluids threatened the Temple's sanctity and order and made profane what was supposed to be holy.

The ancient Greeks were more hysterical* about women being wet and squishy in body *and* mind. Classicist Anne Carson points out that in Greek myths, "Women's boundaries are pliant, porous, mutable. Her power to control them inadequate, her concern for them unreliable... She swells, she shrinks, she leaks."[7] Men, though, were ideally "dry" and able to control both their thoughts and fluids. Heriklitos wrote, "a dry soul is wisest and best," and Homer describes Zeus as having a "dry" mind.[8]

I have become very, very leaky in recent weeks. The ancients would be having a field day with me. I've always been a crier—but a polite one— quick to sniffle when watching commercials, but not breaching the levees. Thanks to my years of theater, I can still cry on cue with three minutes' warning, but it's the weeping equivalent of a golf clap: professional, controlled. During the summer of seminary when I interned as a hospital chaplain I would "empathy cry" with the patients, and sometimes a bit with the other chaplains, but not really "cry," cry. The patients were the ones entitled to big cries, and the other chaplains were tasked with writing

---

* Pun intended.

my assessment for the bishop's committee on ordination. I wanted to maintain professional decorum.

My leakiness is all the more evident against the shriveled, brown autumn landscape of Silicon Valley. The locals call it "gold." Their ancestors came here during the gold rush. It's brown. In the four months I've been here the novelty has begun to wear off. My friends back in D.C. are finishing up the year's legislation. My friends in grad school are in midterms. My friends working in churches are getting ready for Advent. And I'm in California doing…I'm not sure what. All I know is that I've become like an air conditioner on an old car: leaving puddles everywhere I stop. I cry so hard and often that I consider carrying around Gatorade to replenish lost salts.

Maybe, I think, I am just experiencing maturation. I have finished graduate school and moved west. I have a fine job doing meaningful work with smart, funny, collaborative colleagues. My life is, by all accounts, quite nice. But somehow I've become convinced that all adventure is in the past. This is as good as it gets, and I can no longer imagine a future for myself that isn't beige. The projected monotony is devastating. Maybe I'm just a malcontent and will never be happy with my reality.

I spew against inanimate objects. My job has the audacity to end at 5 p.m. each day, leaving me alone with an expanse of solitary time I cannot seem to fill even when I sign up for the adult equivalents of Yearbook and Key clubs.

I really hate my apartment. My disdain is proportional to the appreciation and gratitude I had for the apartment's novelties when I moved in: a community herb garden along the driveway; the upstairs neighbor children who yell to one another in a mishmash of English, Mandarin, and Spanish; the sheer good fortune of an affordable sublet. Now, the windows in my apartment don't close and the upstairs neighbors yell nonstop.

I even hate the sun of Silicon Valley, which has somehow saturated the brains of its residents with unfettered optimism in human innovation and potential. Every nonprofit I encounter seems to sincerely believe that when they succeed in fulfilling their mission statements (which of course they will), the situation they were created to address really will be eradicated.

Silicon Valley seems to lack a healthy sense of sin. Foundational to who we are as human beings is the fact that we will never get the whole picture. We are limited. We cannot innovate our way out of the human condition. Every solution we come up with, no matter how wonderful, will create new, residual issues to contend with. Silicon Valley, though, seems to exude a belief that there will be an iPhone app for that pesky poverty problem. Did no one listen to the end of Steve Jobs' commencement speech?

My family at my college graduation from Yale. Left to right Ellen, Dad (Chris), me, Margo, Mom (Gayle).

Not the part when he said that getting fired was great because it allowed him to innovate, but the part when he said that death was intrinsic to life, and, "Someday not too long from now, you will gradually become the old and be cleared away."[9] I wonder if they've ever heard of the apostle Paul, with his emphasis on inevitable death and human limitations throughout his letters. I long for rain and a release from the relentless optimism.

I call my college roommate Eva during my lunch break at work because I know that she'll pick up (people writing dissertations often accept interruptions that offer human contact) and because she knows tears. Eva and I were given to each other as suitemates as college freshman, and our fate was sealed early.

Late one Thursday night, as our other roommates were preparing for a trip to the pizza dive that notoriously served minors pitchers of Rolling Rock, Eva knocked on my door. She was staying in because she had a paper due the next day and because she'd been having stomach pains. I was in because, as he said good-bye to me, my father had whispered ominously, "Just so you know, I've asked Popou* George to look out for you. He'll be with you everywhere you go." There's nothing like being chaperoned by the ghost of your dead grandfather to put the kibosh on rebellion. Dad had placed the same loving and protective hex on me the first time I went on a date, or traveled alone, or went to a dance. I just couldn't shake the feeling that Popou George would really, really not be down for a dive bar that might be raided by the cops.

---

* Greek: "grandfather."

"Um, I'm really embarrassed, but could you help me figure out how to use this thing?" Eva held a set of directions in one hand and what looked like a folded hairnet in the other. I read the directions and had a minor shame attack for her. "Well," I began as evenly as possible, "This seems to be a poop sieve." I hoped that my tone conveyed the same equanimity as an underwhelmed assessor for *Antiques Roadshow* being shown a Ball mason jar, and not a stool sample kit presented by my college roommate with intestinal issues. After that evening, nothing would be outside the bounds of our friendship, not even her GI tract.

We would become each other's nervous tick barometers. I would ask what was making her chew the inside of her cheek to pulp. She would ask if I had something on my mind when I purchased family-sized boxes of Cheez-Its from the overpriced convenience store.

Eva edited nearly every paper I turned in during my four years of college. She was, I can say with certainty, the only secular Jewish student in our class who majored in French and International Relations while also earning an honorary degree in Latin American Liberation Theology. I was much less academically helpful to her, aside from occasionally writing in her perfect one-inch margins things such as, "Huh? Don't understand this part." Not her fault, I'm sure.

When all the papers were written and edited, she would come into my room and sit on the bright purple futon, purchased from a store that catered to college students—cheap furniture and water pipes. One or the other of us would ask, in an attempt to self-comfort or stabilize, *What if this is as good as it gets?* What if writing a paper that only you and your professor will ever see is the full extent of how our work will impact people? What if all of the rest of our lives we feel as stupid as we do now? What if dating (which neither of us had done in high school) is always so awkward? What if we can never afford a house like the ones we grew up in and we are destined to live in apartments with nail holes plugged with toothpaste? By the end of the night either we decided that if life never got better, then it was still pretty good, or that the best was definitely yet to come.

Many nights Eva cried. Maybe at first she tried to stop the tears. But any such efforts ended by our sophomore year. She would shred limp tissues as her nose ran and the tears fell. I learned to be present in the midst of her sadness, that it was just a part of her. Her tears stopped making me uncomfortable.

Now, a decade later, I am the one crying. I've started having to break down basic tasks into really specific component parts so that I can try to seem like my normal self. Daily life becomes an LSAT logic problem of how Normal Kat would behave:

Problem (1) Normal Kat would respond enthusiastically to this e-mail. I am trying to be normal. Therefore I will convey enthusiasm by using CAPITAL LETTERS and exclamation points (!!!).

Problem (2) Normal Kat would enjoy chatting with her friends at lunch. I am trying to be normal. Therefore, I will ask my friends about themselves, nod as they respond, and offer follow-up questions, such as, "Tell me more about that." I will hold my cup of tea with both hands so that I don't assume my default position of resting my head on the heel of my left hand, eyes staring off into space.

Problem (3) Normal Kat would bring a cheese tray to the party comprised of brie, fruit, and water crackers. I am trying to be Normal Kat. Therefore I will buy those things at the grocery store.

But I get waylaid by annoying transitional steps. Getting a cheese tray would require me to go to the grocery store. So I break it down even further. Normal Kat would get her keys, wallet, and cell phone; get in the car; and drive to the grocery store to buy brie, fruit, and crackers. Therefore, I will pick up my keys…

"I've never felt this way before," I moan to Eva.

"No, it's happened before." The problem with maintaining relationships with people over a long period of time is that they refuse to let you indulge in revisionist history. "Our senior year in college when you broke up with Karl. You asked me if that was how I felt all the time—weepy."

"I'm sorry I asked you that."

"It was a fair question." But it doesn't seem fair, not from this side, or rather what doesn't seem fair was my internal monologue during the years of crying. Even though I was progressive enough to know that she had a disease, just like diabetes or any other chronic condition. That was only what my louder, public voice said on auto-response whenever the topic of mental illness came up in conversation in college. The quieter voice said, *Get your ass up and out of bed already. Maybe this is a coastal thing, that coming from the West or the East you people think you can think about yourselves to the point of immobility, but not me, missy. When you live in the Midwest you learn to get on with it. There's hay to turn.* I have never turned hay. But, still…

"I was never nice enough to you when you were going through this. I wasn't compassionate enough." I tell her.

"Don't worry about it. And I don't mean "don't worry about it" because it's not the time to, but because you did just fine. You were always kind."

Maybe. Maybe not. All I know is that I didn't and wouldn't choose this level of sloppy drippiness and worthlessness; neither would she.

"Is it worse since the funeral?" Eva asks. It's only been a couple weeks since Yiayia died in early November. I didn't see the emotions coming. I nod (not helpful on phone calls.)

The pallbearers were what really got me—the young male cousins and husbands, all in black wool coats and white gloves, looking dapper and straight ahead, like her personal military send-off brigade. They looked almost relieved to have a role, directions, something to do with their hands and eyes. I wanted to watch them in their procession and join them in doing something more than shuffling and crying.

The priests and cantors chanted in the tones I wanted to groan out—minor seconds and thirds of wailing from the bowels. A mountain of a monk with a long braid down his back and a beard down the front recited the Beatitudes in English. Even though the words were spoken, he still emphasized the third-to-last syllable as if he were chanting: "Bleh-sed are THOSE who mourn, for they shall be COMforted. Blessed ARE the meek. For they shall inherIT the earth."

They censed* Yiayia's casket and, then, the whole congregation—declaring all of us holy. The residual incense was so thick that when the sunlight sent diagonal beams across the sanctuary, you could write "WASH ME" in the air and have it hover for just a moment.

Wrists out, I braced my arms against the pew in front of me for the same stability a gymnast would use to mount a pommel horse. Messy tears fell straight onto the carpet below, and embarrassing snot pooled in my sinuses.

Then the monk invited the congregation to pay our final respects at the casket. I watched how the strangers and neighbors paid their respects, so that I'd know how to walk and bow when it was my turn. One by one they leaned over to kiss an icon beside the casket and make some mark of respect—kissing Yiayia's hands, heart, or forehead, or crossing themselves or nodding. When the little cousins came past they covertly tucked pictures and bead necklaces into the casket that they made for her to take with her.

The choir's anthem—really just one person on each voice part, plus the organist, but the whole was greater than the sum of their parts—settled on my shoulders as I stood up, and I was struck with momentary panic. I began to walk toward the icon. I silently begged, "Show me how to do this!" It's the same prayer I offered in college when I walked past the old

---

* The burning of incense to make a time, space, or people set aside for holiness is found throughout religious traditions. In the Christian tradition incense is often burned at key moments in the service, including the reading of the gospel, the communion, and at funerals.

cemetery filled with dead alums who had somehow made it through their rounds of papers and final exams. *You all did it. Show me how.*

But the "it," the "this," was not as clear at the funeral as it was in the streets of a college town. There were no final exams to get through. "Do what?" a bemused voice answered. "Walk across the altar of a church?" "No, I can do *that*." I snapped. I'd seen how everyone else walked across. I followed their lead, balancing on my heels. Up close, the protective glass of the icon was covered in lip marks and streaks. Below was an intricate image of an androgynous person with a gold crown and ruddy skin. In honor of my grandmother, Sophia, they put out an icon of "Sophia," or "Holy Wisdom."

I leaned over, kissed the icon, and said again, "Show me how to do this." "What is 'this'?" the voice pushed. I stood upright, and tears seeped into my mouth. I tasted them and responded to the inner voice, "*This*."

• • •

It's worse since the funeral, but it's not just that. It's the move, and finishing graduate school, and being neither here nor there. And even with the laundry list compiled, I'm not sure why my "Dark Night of the Soul" descended now, though it's likely a combination of chemistry and situation. I can trace behaviors of anxiety and sadness back several generations on both sides of my family. But my ancestors didn't have the luxuries of time and affluence as I do—to just stew on things—which makes the guilt somehow worse. My parents and grandparents didn't work as hard as they did so that I could cry onto my belly. Women didn't fight hard for a place in the workplace, especially the church workplace, so that I could retreat into my shell. The tears all feel very weak.

I'm healthy, educated, living in the developed world, and therefore have access to untold resources. If I become a mother, it won't be for several years. My myriad little cousins are atmospheric contraceptives: reminders of how decibels and finances and time will change—delightfully but permanently—when and if I become a parent. And I have the luxury of choosing—to some extent—when I start a family. This is everything I want, and everything that I imagine my foremothers could want for me, and I'm mush. What could be more selfish or immature?

I tell Eva I feel like I'm faking it at my job, that I look like crap, and that the only thing that seems like a half-solution is eating copious amounts of bread slathered in melted cheese.

Eva asks me what I'm wearing. *Black pants and a pink blouse and black boots.* She asks me if I put on make-up this morning. *Yes.* What kind? *The same as I always do—base, eyeliner, mascara, blush, lipstick.* She asks me to tell her what I *feel* like I'm wearing. *Sweats, unwashed hair in a French braid, no make-up.*

"You don't look how you feel. To everyone else, you look fine—good, even. You feel like a mess, but it's inside. No one else can tell." My mess is hidden. The truth of that is comfort and revelation.

I am so filled with gratitude for her patience and friendship that I cry even harder, alternating, "Thank you," and, "I'm sorry," like I did the night Eva was away, and two of our other roommates set up folding chairs in the bathroom to keep vigil while I expelled my alcohol limits. The next day I bought them potted plants for their dorm windowsills to say thank-you-I'm-sorry-you're-nicer-than-I-am through a low-maintenance flower.

"We've only been on the phone for fifteen minutes," Eva says tenderly. "You've been thinking about how sad and lonely you are all day, but you only just picked up the phone. You've been living with this all day, but you only called fifteen minutes ago, and you haven't derailed my day at all. Before you called, I was thinking about microwaving a burrito for lunch. And, when we hang up, I'll have no trouble microwaving it."

I nod, reassured. "There has to be something good that comes out of all this, right?"

"It will make you more empathetic," Eva offers. "You'll see an expression on someone, and you'll say to yourself: 'Oh, shit. I *know* that look.'"

In Spanish they say that to know someone's sorrow is to "taste it in your own meat." Italians use the phrase to "feel it on your own skin." Deep emotions are supra-sensorial: all of the senses at once and yet uniquely none of them. I try to communicate what my sadness feels like to the people who try to love me but haven't been here before. Words get me only partway there.

Other people who have experienced this sort of sadness have smelled it on their own bed sheets, heard it in their own sighing, seen it in their own reflections. It is like asking what bread tastes like. Bread tastes a bit like pasta or rice or potatoes, but bread is most like…bread. My sadness feels like itself, which adds to its insularity, which is almost but not exactly its own form of selfishness, or at least feels like selfishness. I don't know how to be more inclusive in my description of the dark night of the soul. Having visited the island for a while, maybe I will uniquely see it on someone else's face in the frozen foods section at the grocery store, standing there, unable for some reason to open the industrial freezer door and select a pizza.

The possibility of gaining empathy changes my situation and offers its own sort of hope. I remember conversations with Eva on the purple futon, and the phone calls across the miles since then—countless because they are constant—and I see them ringed in a haze, not so much a dim memorializing as a cloudy lens of incense, declaring her and all our conversations holy.

All Christian traditions maintain that humans are holy and special to God. After all, God became human in Jesus and changed what it meant to be human. The three main Christian traditions, though, interpret a little differently what happened in Jesus becoming human. Like every culture having its own flatbread, each Christianity has its own take on humanity vis-à-vis Jesus.

Protestant traditions tend to emphasize justification—how it is that we as sinners are made right before God. God in pure grace chose to become human, which allows humanity to be made right before God even though we are so, so very wrong. Only by God's grace are we able to have any relationship at all with God. We are not due a relationship with God. What we deserve is alienation or separation from God, but instead God chooses to be in a relationship with us out of love.

Justification frequently emphasizes Jesus' death as the major turning point in humanity's relationship with God. Humanity is on trial before God the Creator for having sinned ever since we were thrown out of Eden in the beginning of Genesis. We are found guilty...but wait! Then Jesus dies on the cross and serves our sentence. God the Creator offers a ruling that since Jesus has served a sentence for all of humanity in all time, being willing to suffer and die on the cross, humanity is made right with God. You get the judge, judged, and punishment all in one convenient "God-man on the cross" package.

A popular phrase in the Protestant justification descriptions is that, apart from the saving work of Jesus, all human beings on their own merits are "a stench in the nostril of God." It's just so severe. And gross. I am also quite aware of my own shortcomings, so to start a relationship with God from the statement, *I really suck, but if you are willing to deign to lower yourself down to measly me...* just doesn't seem to get things off on the right foot.*

Eastern Orthodox Christianity has a different approach, known as deification. In Jesus, humanity is *Dei* (God)-ified. The traditional phrase that the early Christian fathers used to describe deification was, "God made Himself man, that man might become God." We are made into God. Christ's descent into human form made our ascent possible with the Holy Spirit. God becoming human glorifies humanity. Therefore, deification

---

* Justification might be useful for your garden-variety narcissist who thinks herself pretty amazing all the time and could afford to be a little humbled, but, then again, she wouldn't recognize the doctrine as applying to her anyway.

emphasizes Jesus's birth as a human. But somehow the idea that we become God-ified also doesn't sit right with me. I'm too Protestant to go along with it. I am so, so *not* God.

Roman Catholic theology tends to take a third track: sanctification, in which Jesus made all of humanity and everything about humanity holy and precious to God. Theologian Karl Rahner describes how through Jesus everything about us is infused with Godself. Thanks to Jesus, when God creates humanity, God does not "produce something different from himself in the [human] creature, but rather he communicates his own divine reality and makes it a constitutive element in the fulfillment of the creature."[10] We are imbued or infused with Godself—God's own divine reality—in our very cells. God communicates Godself to us in free, pure love, and ever after humanity is changed. We are made holy, but not exactly God-ified. I can get behind that.

Rahner's take highlights how we are sanctified rather than simply justified to "always emphasize that we become and are God's children through God's grace, that in justification the Holy Spirit is given to us, that we are the temple of God,...anointed and beloved of God through God's grace."[11] Our very bodies are sanctified and holy. Tears or blood, gastrointestinal symptoms or the chewed inside skin of a cheek—none of this is an abomination to God, or unholy. Everything about us is, was, and will be touched by Godself.

Pacing the sidewalk in Palo Alto, trying to remain an object in motion and not trip over my own feet, Rahner resonates. I'm not God, but neither am I totally depraved. That I'm not defiled or a failure, that Eva came through this same sort of sadness and so might I, is hope enough. And, someday, when I see my own expression of despair on someone else's face, that too will be an opportunity for sanctification. Because of Christ, nothing is outside the love of God, not tears or the inability to select a frozen pizza or the ways in which we so desperately need one another. It's all radiantly holy, holy, holy.

Discussion Questions:

- Did you ever have a difficult period or situation in your own life that eventually led you to be able to have empathy for someone else? If so, did this change how you feel about that difficult time?
- Between justification, deification, and sanctification, which makes the most sense to you?
- The author goes to extremes to say that no bodily fluid or function is too gross for God. How do you feel about the human body?

6

Oh, Christ on the Cross
The Crucifixion

I have a lot of cross jewelry—a small gold cross from my confirmation, a silver cross from Jerusalem for my high school graduation, a wooden cross from a college friend who lived in Guatemala, and many, many crosses from my time in divinity school. They mostly sit in the jewelry box. In small part this is because I'm not wild about visual proselytizing, though I'm never put off by another person of faith wearing a headscarf or turban or skullcap. I'm actually prone to see them and think, "We probably have a lot in common, considering that we're both religiously observant."*

The larger part is I just don't like the symbol of the cross itself. It represents the most violent, painful part of the Christian story. The hero is killed in a rigged political charade. The cross was a symbol of public execution. I may as well wear a tiny silver guillotine or noose or electric chair. I hate that Jesus' execution, not his birth or life as a human, is what's memorialized in Christianity's main symbol.

Why not a baby?

A: Baby on a chain is way creepier.

How about da Vinci's medical human diagram in which the guy looks like he's in a jumping jack web?

---

* Then I start to think, we both take prayer breaks during the day (though the person with the head covering probably is more diligent than me). We both have foods we choose to abstain from (okay, not really me unless it's Lent and I've done some version of Weight Watchers for Jesus that year). We both adhere to an alternate calendar (though really my high holidays are federal holidays). You're probably actually a better, more observant person of faith, oh person of the religious head covering. *Darn.*

A: Too late historically, and also already claimed by the medical community.

What about just a block of wood? Jesus as carpenter?

A : Too Cub Scouts.

Really? The cross? What kind of religion is this, always coming back to pain and suffering? Shouldn't suffering be eliminated if we're doing this human project right and following all the rules of the faith? Give me butterflies and rainbows and prerecorded laugh tracks. Who thought that the cross was a good marketing scheme? Or a good theological claim?

At different points in history, theologians have emphasized the crucifixion as central to the Christian narrative. Sometimes it's been the climactic moment of God's triumph over death, God's victory over evil, or God's solidarity with those who suffer. Always, though, the crucifixion is essential to the story of how humanity is reconciled to God. We're stuck with these two rough blocks of wood in our narrative. Somehow the pain is part of the way things work out—the mystery. We just don't get the Christian story of reconciliation without the pain of the crucifixion.

The pain and suffering I'm going through in my autumn malaise is so, so not colossal or monumental to the outside observer. But, I decide, it's more than I can healthily navigate on my own. I suck up my pride and call my friend and neighbor Emily to ask for the number of the therapist she and her fiancé have used in the past. I guess I'm lucky that I know people in therapy, so I don't have to start from Google. But that's sort of like saying, "It's great that so many of your friends know insurance adjusters, considering that your house burned down." I'd rather not have the house on fire to begin with.

• • •

I really don't want to call Emily. When she answers, I think of hanging up or throwing up. It's weird, because this is not my first time getting counseling, and I've always really loved it in the past. The first time, though, that was totally Ross Perot's fault. Because I'm evolved and self-aware and own my own inclinations, I feel completely at ease chalking my entire six-year-old experience with Rorschach blots up to that little man with big ears and an even bigger Napoleon complex.

Plano, Texas, where I spent many years of my childhood, is the world headquarters for Electronic Data Systems (now part of Hewlett Packard), Perot's multi-million dollar company. During my first and second grade years, from 1986 through 1988, Perot served as head of the Selection

Committee on Public Education, which instituted statewide testing standards. Perot's panel established basic proficiency standards and elements of merit pay as a way to ensure quality education for Texan children. This included standardized testing throughout elementary school. If you've met a group of six- or seven-year-olds recently, note that they have a wide range of abilities when it comes to simply holding pencils and filling in answer bubbles, much less doing written analysis of reading passages. Tensions ran high throughout my elementary school during the inaugural launch of this testing program. Between the three first-grade classrooms of twenty students each, a full fourteen antsy boys were medicated for Attention Deficit Disorder by the end of the school year.

I remember my first grade teacher thrusting a list of 130 spelling and vocabulary words at me and threatening: "You'd better score well on these for the way you talk." At that age, I had advanced language capabilities—far above and beyond my own reading level—because I was read to. In listening to stories I fell in love with language—with *language*, but not with *reading* itself.

Read words seemed a different universe altogether. Words on a page had too many variables. The way words looked and what they meant and how they sounded were all different codes to me. One didn't seem to have much to do with another. Speaking has always been easier for me than reading or writing. I figure things out by talking about them. At the end of a discussion session during which I'd made some fine contributions, a college professor once handed me back a paper with a really poor grade and remarked, "You're much cleverer than you come across on paper."

I couldn't master the spelling and vocabulary words. It was clear to me that I wasn't measuring up. I developed full-blown insomnia.

Fantasy and reality still blend in first grade.* Insomnia took on a whole anthropomorphic existence, as if a Saturday morning cartoon villain jumped out of the storyboard and under my bed. I could sense him prowling around, beginning in the late afternoon. I imagined him scoping out the seams of the cement foundation around the house where the fire ants homesteaded. He lurked beside the rumbling air conditioner compressor under my parent's bedroom window and behind the can of WD40 in the garage. By dinnertime, I wanted to pace, just to keep him from settling.

He didn't like onions sautéing or people talking, so he stayed away during dinner itself. But then he started to cloud the edges of the bathroom

---

* Some of you are probably reading this whole book thinking that fantasy and reality never stopped blending together for me. A fair point, but it was more widespread and pronounced in early elementary school.

mirror while I brushed my teeth. He'd make a partial retreat during stories and prayers, only to return in full force when my parents leaned in to kiss me goodnight.

"One more thing!" I'd protest. "I forgot to tell you something about my day." The only way to keep Insomnia away was to not be the only person awake. He didn't care for company.

"Katie, everyone has to go to sleep now," a parent would answer. "You don't have to actually sleep, but you do have to stay in your room."

I'd lie in bed for what seemed like hours. When I couldn't stand it any longer, I'd creep into the living room to see if light was still coming from under my parents' bedroom door. If there was light, I'd lie on the floor where I could see the light, hoping to fall asleep before the light went out. Once the light disappeared, I watched the digital clock on the VCR flip number after number. I knew that I was supposed to be getting a good night's sleep to do well in school, but I just couldn't sleep.

I often slipped into my younger sister Ellen's twin bed to listen to her breathe. Today she sleeps surrounded by huge pillows on every side, which I attribute to the years of being scrunched in by me. Sometimes I woke my parents up so that someone else would be awake, and Insomnia would leave. It was worth it to me to deal with my parents' fury at being awakened, yet again, to not be alone with Insomnia.

My saving grace during those years came in the form of Janet, a frizzy-haired woman with Coke-bottle glasses who smelled of old coffee percolated with garlic. She had me make things with Play-Doh and look at ink blots. Then she told my mother what every parent of a child who seems abnormal wants to hear: that there wasn't anything wrong with me. I was just really sensitive to the ambient stress of the public school system's overhaul.

I can be high strung. School testing brought it out early. As much as I'd like to demonize Ross Perot, my condition wasn't his fault, though he helped surface the issues pretty early on. And, to the guy's credit, his statewide testing in Texas served as the basis for his education platform in the 1992 presidential campaign and made standardized education goals a topic of national conversation.

Janet supplied me with some coping skills, which is really what my best experiences with therapy have done. She gave me concrete tools for when Insomnia and other personal demons start to rear up. My parents put timers on my lamps so that I didn't have to turn the light off and could just fall asleep drawing, or, later, reading. No clocks were visible from my bed. I ritualistically turned the alarm clock to face the wall each night. I checked that the alarm was set three times, though I didn't do this in any special rhythm. It's somehow important to me to write that last phrase, to have you know that I didn't check the clock in a certain rhythm. That's one of the insidious aspects of mental health. Like prisoners having a hierarchy of who's a really bad criminal, I want to make very clear that I wasn't, like, *really* extreme in my controlling tendencies. I just needed to check the alarm clock three times, not in rhythm. Please, rhythms are for people who are really off. Can I get a high-five to that? Anyone? *Anyone?* Okay, no.

On the bedside table, I kept a notepad upon which I would draw or later write all of the things I was anxious about; I promised myself that if I put them on paper, I would deal with them the next day. In high school the list was color- and symbol-coded. If I highlighted something in blue it had to get done that day. A sun to the right-hand side meant that I had to do it before noon; a star, before I came home from school. Sometimes I would begin to drift off to sleep and pop awake to reprioritize suns and stars and blue bars.

Later, my mom read about a hydrotherapy technique in which I would run my wrists under cold water for thirty seconds. I alternated moving my wrists under the direct stream while counting so that each wrist got equal exposure, if you must know. Then I'd dry them quickly and lay in bed on my side with my hands stuck under my arms a la Mary Katherine Gallagher on *Saturday Night Live*. The concept was that chilling the pulse points pulled blood away from your head and slowed down thinking and your pulse rate. Sometimes it worked—*works*. I no longer have to do these things nightly, but when I have a lot going on, the color-coding and hydrotherapy return.

As much detail as I've given here, I only went to see Janet four times. She was a pro who helped in short order.

I became a very public evangelist as an undergraduate for the free therapy offered by Yale when I thought that some of my friends could use a dose of head-shrinking. Therapy was like an extracurricular for me. It was free! We talked about me! I was sad when the end of my sessions with my perpetually jolly Italian practitioner ended. He told me the same things my family and friends did, but I believed him because he didn't have to be nice.

I had no impact, though, on a small woman with a big drinking problem, or the girl who walked into my room holding a pregnancy test in one hand and a bottle of green hair dye in the other and blurted out, "Which should I do first?" and then ran out of the room before I could answer. She returned several hours later with her nose pierced and never mentioned the pregnancy test again.

One might think that with a history of voluntarily going to therapy and learning coping mechanisms, I'd be down with my down self and "get thee to a therapist in California." Um, no. I'd certainly advise friends to do that, and parishioners even more so, but the words I speak aloud are not the script I hear in my head. I don't want this reality. I want to be completely fine and functional and independent and well. I don't even pack suitcases I can't lift into the overhead compartment, because I sure as hell don't want to need help.

It feels like failure, like I'm too weak to get through life pulling up my own bootstraps. I would never say this to someone who was hurting, but it is my perpetual in-head reel.

The therapist that my friend Emily recommends is only available for an intake session on my twenty-ninth birthday. I hear the voice of an old, wizened Greek woman* *tsking* in my head: "That is *not* a good sign. You do not do that to start out a new year." But the therapist turns out to be wicked smart, kind, and (as an added bonus) an ordained minister. He describes things first in psychological principles and then using biblical tenets, which totally works for me. Therapists are like good music teachers or coaches insofar as they have to be a good fit, and that I have trust that, in their area of expertise, they are smarter than I am.

I explain to the new therapist that everything feels "amorphous" here in California. The culture and geography are unfamiliar. My family is far away, and so is the structure of academia that I knew. I don't know what I'm supposed to be doing for these next two years. There's no specific goal I'm working toward, and I feel untethered when I'm not working toward something.

My therapist tilts his head, and suggests, "It's possible that someday you'll see this wandering time as a gift. Maybe God is saying, 'Lean on me. I'm the one thing that's constant.'"

Perhaps.

The therapist gives me drills for dealing with changes and surprises, so that when called upon to navigate life's ups and downs, I'll have the basic building blocks in place. For weeks I begin each morning writing, "Today I will be surprised. I will consider the surprise," seven times in a spiral notebook before leaving for work. Lo and behold, I am indeed surprised everyday, but it's less assaulting when I can know it's coming. I'm just grateful to have something tangible to do. Calling him felt like a step; so did showing up; and now he's given me homework. Each of these

---

* The voice sounds uncannily like the ghost of Grandma Tzeitel in *Fiddler on the Roof*.

three things feels really monumental in terms of doing something on the road to better.

• • •

In a Venn diagram of foods that I eat and foods that my friend Emily's fiancé eats, pizza is one of the only things in the overlap category. We frequently go for pizza together. So when Emily invites me out for my birthday at a pizza joint, my ever-gracious internal response is, "Really? For my birthday we can't go somewhere that doesn't deal in the currency of mozzarella and marinara, even though it might inconvenience your boyfriend?" I almost cancel at the last minute, but Normal Kat wouldn't cancel. (Then again, Normal Kat also wouldn't critique an invitation. *Baby steps.*)

I debate long and hard about changing out of my mismatched weekend clothes. It's just a pizza place, and I don't even really want to go. My quest for normalcy gets to me change into something slightly more presentable, though with an elastic waistband, so that I still feel like I'm in my PJs. Too much clothing constriction could take me under.

I enter the restaurant: a chain that tries to make rental space in a California strip mall feel like a neighborhood tavern, with pre-engraved oak tables and floors not fully swabbed at the end of the night so that beer stickiness builds up. I look around for Emily and Matt.

There, incongruously, against the wall, are my coworkers at the nonprofit and friends from college and church and a neighbor. It is just about everyone I know in California. "Surprise!" They yell.

"Holy shit." I respond. I do an uncanny impersonation of Sally Fields' Oscar acceptance speech in my head. "You like me! You really like me!" But aloud, all I can articulate is, "Thank you." Emily whispers, "Matt and I thought you might need this."

I did. I never in a million years would have asked for a surprise party for my twenty-ninth birthday when I was heavily in sweatpants mode and just beginning my course of therapy, but it was exactly what I needed.

• • •

"Can you see," asks my therapist, "how this time is a vital part of your preparation for ministry?"

"Sure," I shrug, all Eeyore-like, "I'll be better with other anxious and depressed people."

"Yes, but can you imagine how often you'll encounter people who are facing something bigger than they can handle on their own? Because that's what this is for you."

I will keep paying this man.

I don't want to laud and elevate suffering because that leads to all sorts of martyrdom celebration, but there is a reality of suffering—in our stories and in our stories with God. And there is beauty and grace within the suffering: I find a good therapist for me right off the bat. My parents loan me money to pay for my sessions. Eva takes my calls. Emily and Matt throw me a party.

And it wouldn't have been nearly so beautiful or poignant or mysterious in timing but for the preceding pain. That's the thing about the end of the Christian story—the beautiful mystery of God and humanity reconciled in Christ is always hard-won and always hard-wrought and always comes out of some sort of pain.

I would rather read about myself in a case study than be myself on the hard days. I'd like to develop third-person sympathy for the character in pain. Second best would be having a "gold star holiness perspective" to be able to be authentically grateful for every aspect of who I am and the entirety of my experience here on earth. I'm not there.

I do my best to lean into God and ask for help with living through something bigger than what I can do alone. That'll have to be enough for now.

Discussion Questions:

- Can you tell about an experience of your own suffering (be it mental health or otherwise)?
- Does your perception of someone change if/when you know that they've struggled with mental health issues?
- What is the most compelling Christian symbol for you?
- What is the most important part of the Jesus story for you (birth, life, death, resurrection, etc.)?
- Why does suffering exist?

Apocalypse in the Tropics
End Times

It's winter in Silicon Valley, which means almost daily rain. Rainbows break through the clouds more often than lightning does. The land receives the entire year's precipitation in just a couple months' time. Reservoirs swell to bursting. The schools and malls are all designed with outdoor passageways, so people scurry and squeal between appointments. From the time my bishop in Connecticut e-mails me to set up a phone call to the time I decide that it's so obviously God's will that I go to the Dominican Republic is maybe a week.

Initially, when I receive the e-mail, I'm panicked. The guy never calls. Has he heard through the grapevine that I've been struggling emotionally or that I'm not as involved as I could be at the neighborhood church? I decide that no, he hasn't heard anything. The only other alternative I can think of—why he'd call and not just email -- is that he must need another female chaperone for the diocesan youth mission trip to the Dominican Republic. While I wouldn't be thrilled to give up one of my two weeks of vacation at the nonprofit where I'm now working to go back to the Dominican, and youth skills aren't my forte, I start to think that going back to the Caribbean with a bunch of Connecticut teenagers wouldn't be the worst thing in the world. Maybe a mission trip is just the thing I need. I could use a little apocalypse.

The term *apocalypse* literally means "unveiling," or, as it is often translated into English, "revelation." An apocalypse is a story or experience in which we are given a truer, deeper understanding of reality. We emerge from apocalypses with an altered notion of our world and our role in it.[12]

We know plenty of apocalypse stories. Charles Dickens's *A Christmas Carol* is apocalyptic; Scrooge is shown his life in a different light through his travels with the ghosts of Christmas past, present, and future. And he emerges from the experience with a commitment to change his relationship to Bob Cratchit and the other poor families in his community.

Dorothy in *The Wizard of Oz* sees her life in Depression-era Kansas differently following her time with the Munchkins, the Scarecrow, and the Wicked Witch of the West. She comes back to good old Kansas with a new appreciation for the people who care for her.

The Bible is chock-full of apocalypse stories. Jesus tells his followers an apocalypse story in Luke 16, about a rich man who treats a poor man named Lazarus horribly throughout their lives. Both men die. The rich man is taken to Hades, while Lazarus ends up at the side of the Hebrew Scriptures rock star, Abraham. The rich man begs Abraham to send Lazarus to warn the rich man's family of their fate if they don't shape up, but Abraham answers that his family is beyond convincing (presumably, Jesus' audience was not).

In the book of Revelation, the author takes the Jewish community living under imperialist Rome on a voyage in which they see Rome as a fear-mongering, power-hungry overlord, but one who won't have ultimate power over the struggling Judeo-Christian community.

The point of these stories is that the readers or the participants see what is and what could be, and gain the conviction that they have the power to change the future. In this way, apocalypse stories parallel the Hebrew Scripture prophets. They tell what is now, and foretell what could be, while always giving the participants an opportunity to impact that future. Hebrew Scriptures scholar Yehezkel Landau writes, "Biblical prophecy is not a foretelling of inevitable doom or destruction. Rather it is a timely warning combined with promise." The outcome is never a sure-fire thing but rather conditional, like a choose-your-own adventure ending for the Israelites, "dependent on human behavior in response to God's word."[13]

Apocalyptic experiences and prophetic statements are like a Type II diabetes diagnosis: you could lose your eyesight, your feet, and end up on dialysis; *or* you could change your lifestyle and your relationship to your body, to the earth, to the people around you, and keep your independence. Apocalypses are meant to wake readers up to urgency and agency in the present world.

Mission trips are ideal settings for apocalypses. You're outside of normal life. You're with new people in a new culture. The last mission trip I went on, my last summer of divinity school, was completely apocalyptic... and *hot*—so God-awful hot.

I had been told to dress extremely modestly as a missionary chaperone. In long cotton skirts, close-toed shoes, modest blouses, small earrings, and no make-up, I looked every bit the observant female. With a well-placed headscarf or wig I could have blended into Riyadh or Tel Aviv without a hitch. By the time our diesel minibus rolled up to the windowless cinderblock building where we would spend our days, our backs and legs were soaked in sweat.

The Church Mothers—Dominican ladies in clingy knit tops and Jolly Rancher-colored jeans so tight that they kept their cell phones nestled in their cleavage—gestured for us to come in, come in. There, spread out in immense hospitality, were tiny cups full of steaming hot, syrupy sweet Dominican coffee. Dixie Cups were developed to help stop the spread of tuberculosis while taking communion at churches in the American South, and I have never been so grateful for the TB epidemic. I forced a smile and took a sip of coffee. The Connecticut teens followed suit. They were really good kids.

Several dozen Dominican children had already crept into the 14' x 14' cement room before we got to the bottom of the Dixie cups. "So," the head Mother asked me, "What are your plans for the children this week? We are here to assist."

I smiled at her modesty, "No, no. We are here to serve *you*."

Startled, she shook her head and stated firmly, "We were told to open the church and that you all were coming to run a camp for the neighborhood all week." I looked at my co-chaperone in panic. The retired Air Force officer-turned-bachelor-investment-banker was pushing seventy-five, and he was in heaven. This week of leading Connecticut teens on a mission trip in the Dominican Republic was his retirement *raison d'être*. My gender and barely passable Spanish made me his perfect co-chaperone for that year's trip. I had little choice. He'd called on behalf of the bishop's office of the Episcopal Diocese of Connecticut. When one is in the Episcopal ordination process, and someone from the bishop's office calls to ask a favor, there is one acceptable answer: I can only hope that I'm a tissue match.

The bachelor/banker was hi-fiving Dominican toddlers and trying to get a game of "Ring Around the Rosie" going. *"Que dice?"* the children asked each other, *What's he saying?*

Oh children, he sings a song of the Bubonic Plague, which had much the same effect as the small pox that my missionary forefathers brought to this land, inadvertently killing many of your ancestors. Come, let us frolic.

The eight teens from Connecticut were backed up against the cement walls unsure of what to do. That made nine of us.

The Church Mothers divided the neighborhood children into two groups—an indoor Bible lesson/craft group and an outdoor group that would play games in the alley outside. I head outside while my co-chaperone takes the indoor shift. Outdoors the colorfully painted concrete walls seemed to sweat children. Small, agile brown bodies crept out from crevices between buildings and dropped down from corrugated metal roofs. They sidled up in packs from both sides of the alley. *"Americana! Americana!"* they yelled from every direction. Older Dominican girls remained in the shadows, pushing their charges toward me— a polar bear in the tropics. I grabbed the two hands nearest to me and tried to make a circle and explain "Duck, Duck, Goose" in broken Spanish,to no avail. Finally a boy took pity on me, grabbed a beach ball from my bag and yelled, "Game with ball!" The children cheered and organically formed teams of dust and bare feet. The older girls receded further back into the shadows, their younger siblings and cousins relatively safe.

We ran ourselves thirsty, but when I led the children inside to do crafts, the Church Mothers meted out a single Dixie Cup of juice per child. "More, more," the little Olivers begged. "No more," the Mothers answered decisively, and handed me my own liter of water. When I began to pour it into the children's cups they took my bottle away from me. *There isn't enough for everyone. And if you don't drink, they don't have a camp.* Ah, the crappy ethics of relative affluence.

Next, the Church Mothers sat all of the children around tiny tables, some two to a chair. They read the Bible story aloud from cheap black-and-white photocopy packets. I roamed to keep order during story time. Even though I tried to soften the effect with smiles and gentle touch, my verb tenses made me sound like a petty theocratic dictator. A rough English translation would have sounded something like: *"Silence, child! Your teacher attempts to speak of Bible. If capable of reading, demonstrate such to myself by point your finger to right words in booklet. There will be silence at now."* I was a Christianized Kim Jong-il, though with a bit less animatronic panda.

Just before the end of the Bible lesson, a Church Mother beckoned me over to the craft table. She stood spread-eagled in front of the craft table, cell phone rising between her breasts as she raised her arms to guard the craft table with a full body block. "Like this," she instructed. "The church children know how to behave, but the others, they have no manners. They will steal and then nothing is left for the rest of the week." I didn't know one child from another, churched from neighborhood. To me they were all children in summer camp.

With that the Bible lesson ended. Tiny hands darted under my arms and around my waist to play in the metallic shreds on the table behind me. I longed to let them glitter gorge themselves like little RuPauls, but we had to make the craft supplies last all week. Who knew that glitter was an even more valuable commodity than water? The teens helped the children write their names while the Church Mothers tried to find patches of breeze to dry the glue. The air clouded with glitter and yarn shreds.

At three o'clock the Church Mothers called out some semblance of, "You must now go to your homes." The children surged against my craft table body block grabbing for any and all supplies on their way out. Then, as if the stagehands had pulled down a new scrim, the children were gone, and only the Americans and Church Mothers remained, sweeping glitter and shreds of paper with push brooms into the street. The van from the bishop's office sidled up, and we piled in.

There was morning. There was evening. The first day.

Each day the children became more and more individual to us, and we to each other. The older Dominican girls morphed into our helpers and translators. When the American teen girls sat down at the tiny tables for the Bible study lesson, one or two children would curl into their laps while others braided and twisted and knotted their hair into Midsummer Night's Dream confections. The American teen boys pulled pummeling little boys off each other in their soccer referee duties.

One evening back at the dorms, in the shower hour between the day camp and dinner, a teen sought me out in the stairwell. She was a dancer and a dead ringer for Audrey Hepburn. She burst into tears, "I just don't understand. We're here for a week and this junk, this cheap stuff we brought down in our suitcases is bringing these kids so much joy and we have so much back in Connecticut. I just don't get why the world is the way it is. What's the point?"

The point of the trip, I think, was that very moment and others like it: when the teens asked those questions, and when they were overcome by what they'd seen. Providing an awakening—an opportunity to see the world with new eyes—is exactly what youth mission trips attempt to do. The fruit of that trip to the Dominican Republic is only now bearing out, as the teens who went on the trip are graduating from college and entering adulthood. Two of them have decided to become high school Spanish teachers, and both attribute their decision to that trip. Teaching a foreign language doesn't alleviate poverty immediately, but it demonstrates an awareness of others and a commitment to experience someone else's reality through their words.

• • •

So, here I am, thinking that maybe God's response to my recent messiness is that God has been opening me up to the possibility of doing international mission again. By the time the bishop calls, I am in a full-blown tizzy of missional enthusiasm. I'm so amped that I don't trust myself to take the call from a Starbucks. Instead I hold am umbrella in one hand, cell phone in the other, and power walk around the perimeter of a park that, in nice weather, is home to many people who are otherwise homeless, but in the rain is home only to birds. I am ready not just to chaperone a week in the Dominican—I could quit my job or take vacation or an extended leave to be a crappy translator somewhere. Without the last couple months of weepiness, I might not have been open to being sent alone overseas before, but now, who loves malaria pills? This girl.

The bishop makes the mistake of beginning our phone call with the question, "How are you doing?" I respond with the overbearing enthusiasm of a Zig Ziglar motivational speaker. I am better than fantastic! (*Why? What have you heard?*) God is giving me the opportunity to learn so much about fundraising and the church landscape in the Bay Area, and I'm in a fantastic small group at a local Evangelical church and teaching Sunday school at the Episcopal Church. *And did I mention that I'm doing great?*

We keep chatting and chatting. He's giving nothing. I start throwing him softballs. I mention that I've been struck by the large Spanish-speaking community in the Bay Area and have started to volunteer in English as a Second Language tutoring. I just participated in a Habitat for Humanity build day. I'm a confirmation sponsor to a junior high girl at the church whose family is going through a hard time.

Still nothing. Finally, I ask if there's anything in particular he wanted to talk about, anything he wants me to do?

Nope, he says. He just wanted to call and check in and let me know that I'm cared for, that my home diocese is praying for me. He tells me that it sounds like I'm doing good things to find my place in that community and to prepare for the priesthood. He ends the calls saying that he'll keep me in prayer.

No. No! No! This is where he's supposed to be my Bishop in Shining Armor who is so holy that he intuitively knows just when to call me up out of the blue and send me to a poverty-stricken country to escape my own reality. Let's try this again. I say, "Is there anything else?" And you, Mr. Bishop Man, say, "Why, yes, Kat. I've been praying on this for quite some time, and I'd really like you to consider the possibility of a radical departure..." Then I say, very reverently, "I will pray on this." Then I call right back and accept. Got it?

I am disappointed, to say the least. But I'm more than a little chagrined when I realize that I hadn't wanted want an apocalypse after all. I'd wanted a *Rapture*—a permanent escape from my present reality.

Throughout Christian history,* but especially in the last 150 years in the United States and England, a particular distortion of apocalyptic scripture has taken hold, known as Rapture theology. "Rapture Mongers" focus on Revelation chapter 20, right at the high point of battle, in which the Roman overlords are about to be axed by the God of the Judeo-Christians.

Then I saw an angel coming down from heaven, holding in his hand the key to the bottomless pit and a great chain. He seized the dragon, that ancient serpent, who is the Devil and Satan, and bound him for a thousand years, and threw him into the pit, and locked and sealed it over him, so that he would deceive the nations no more, until the thousand years were ended. After that he must be let out for a little while.

Then I saw thrones, and those seated on them were given authority to judge. I also saw the souls of those who had been beheaded for their testimony to Jesus and for the word of God. They had not worshiped the beast or its image and had not received its mark on their foreheads or their hands. They came to life and reigned with Christ a thousand years. (The rest of the dead did not come to life until the thousand years were ended.) This is the first resurrection. Blessed and holy are those who share in the first resurrection. Over these the second death has no power, but they will be priests of God and of Christ, and they will reign with him a thousand years. (20:1–6)

A goodly amount of paranoid pencil** and thought has gone into figuring out exactly the date and time of these thousand-year periods so that true believers can be ready for the Second Coming of Christ.

The problem is that Rapture Mongers stop reading Revelation at chapter 20 and conveniently never get to the end of the story, chapter 21, when John of Patmos, the author, reassures his Roman Judeo-Christian community that God loves the world and is in the world:

---

* For example, a separatist sect known as the Manicheans in the earliest years of Christianity. According to the Manicheans, the world was evil, filled with the scourge of Satan, and the goal of Christians was to escape the world and leave it behind to stew in its own evil juices.

** Not to mention yards and yards of plastic wrap to line basement fallout rooms, stocked with cans of spam because apparently the antichrist won't be able to penetrate plastic or aluminum. In a great cosmic battle, Jesus' biggest foe might be botulism.

Then I saw a new heaven and a new earth; for the first heaven and the first
earth had passed away, and the sea was no more. And I saw the holy city, the
new Jerusalem, coming down out of heaven from God, prepared as a bride
adorned for her husband. And I heard a loud voice from the throne saying,
    "See, the home of God is among mortals.
    He will dwell with them;
    they will be his peoples,
    and God himself will be with them;
    he will wipe every tear from their eyes." (21:1–4)

God returns to dwell among God's people, on the earth, in chapter 21.
God is with them, and us, living and moving on our earth. The kingdom
of heaven is a present and future promise, and throughout it God has and
will dwell in the world that God created and loves.

Therein lies Christian hope: that we participate in God's work on
earth—this earth, here and now—even as we hope for a future we cannot
see. Christianity is oriented toward a "Due North" full of hope, which is
what invigorates our present lives.

There is something so attractive about escape, about the possibility
of being whisked away to a paradise where there's none of this life's junk.
Perhaps coincidentally, or perhaps not, Rapture theology experienced a
huge surge in popularity immediately following the Civil War. As I mentioned in the chapter on interpreting scripture, abolition caused a crisis
in American Christian communities because both those who supported
slave holding *and* abolitionists found scriptural support for their positions.
The text-based disagreements undermined the notion of scripture only
ever having one meaning for a given situation. Also, America was gener-
ally broken after the Civil War. Americans had no idea how on earth they
would possibly knit themselves together across ideological and racial and
geographic lines. Rapture theology offered a way out of having to do any
of that hard work of coming together. An immediate end time meant that
they didn't have to repair their post-Bellum selves. African American abo-
litionist Sojourner Truth commented on the Rapture theology:

> You seem to be expecting to go to some parlor away up somewhere, and
> when the wicked have been burnt, you are coming back to walk in tri-
> umph over their ashes—this is to be your New Jerusalem!! Now I can't see
> anything so very nice in that, coming back to such a muss as that will be, a
> world covered with the ashes of the wicked. Besides, if the Lord comes and
> burns—as you say he will—I am not going away; I am going to stay here

and stand the fire, like Shadrach, Meshach, and Abednego!* And Jesus will walk with me through the fire, and keep me from harm.[14]

The Rapture didn't arrive before the United States began to address slavery, and the Rapture didn't arrive after 9/11, and—much to my disappointment—the Rapture doesn't arrive in 2009. Instead, God comes into the midst of everything to walk with us through the difficult post-bellum eras of our lives.

God's apocalypses do not remove us from the world but rather help us root more deeply. When asked what he would do if he found out that the end times were going to arrive the next day, Martin Luther famously replied, "I would plant a tree." To be a Christian in this world is to invest in it. The Christian life is made up of us and God in this very place—digging in deeply, not escaping from it. Jesus walks with us through the fires and the problem solving. He doesn't vacuum us up, up, and away from them, which sometimes totally sucks** because then we're still stuck in our earthly lives.

Well, shoot. I'm going to have to stay where I've been planted and have my own apocalyptic reorientation right where I am. Full body removal into an alternative universe would have been much more exciting.

Discussion Questions:

• Has your worldview ever changed through travel?
• Was there ever a time during which you hoped that some event would take place to let you escape the present?
• How do you understand the difference between *apocalypse* and *Rapture*? Is it an important difference?

---

* Characters in the Hebrew Scriptures book of Daniel, which is itself an apocalypse story, not a Rapture tale.
** Pun intended.

8

Bubble Girl
The Trinity

Picture what you think buildings at Yale look like: maybe stone gothic or colonial Georgian with beautiful fireplaces and snifters of bourbon.

Now picture what would happen if a fifth grade boy was given a piece of graph paper and a protractor and told to design the world's most elaborate ant farm, rampant with multilayer dead-end tunnels just to confuse the ants. Build a four-story mold from his model and fill it with wet concrete. Poke a couple of air holes in it for windows. Then spray it with mildew and Soviet communist malaise. That was my dorm. For *four* years.

Given the choice between colonial Georgian and Soviet insect farms, most people would choose Option A. But only legacies—that is, children or siblings of Yalies, can choose to live in the beautiful dorms their relatives lived in. The rest of us got the leftovers, including the weird 1970s architectural experiments. Most of my college friends lived in my dorm and were the first in their families to go to a place like Yale—many the first to go to college in the United States.

Yes, I went to Yale, but I'm the legacy of scrappy Chicago characters straight out of central casting for the Ellis Island immigrant experience. My dad's side, the Greek side, started out washing dishes and laying railroad ties at the turn of the century, and then moved on to owning Greek diners and working in factories. My mom's dad was an Irish Chicago cop and a Democratic precinct captain under the first Mayor Daley. His father was an Irish Chicago cop who died in a steam bath "accident," and his mother was a shirtwaist factory worker.

My parents put themselves through city college but vowed from the moment they conceived of conceiving that their kids would go away to school. "Sleep-away college" meant having the experience of living in a dorm, period. I applied to only one school outside of the Midwest, just on a whim.

My mom responded to my Yale acceptance letter, "Well, honey, you'll always be able to know that you were accepted to Yale."

"Mama, I want to go there."

"But we didn't save for that."

"But you told me to apply."

"I told you you *could* apply. We never thought you'd get in."

It is a function of being human, and particularly an eighteen-year-old human, that we make decisions without being able to see their full impact. I was unaware, and necessarily so, of what it had taken for my parents to save as much as they had, and equally ignorant of what working three work-study jobs at a time and taking on student loans would really mean. I accepted my unlikely offer with the wonderful combination of faith and obstinacy possible in teenagehood—kind of like Mary, the mother of Jesus.

One of my parents' friends, a journalist and community organizer, gave me a high school graduation card with a shark's tooth inside. The card read, "I just learned a new word this week—*talisman*. It means a good luck charm. Take this shark's tooth with you as a talisman of where you came from, a reminder to have adventures and to come back to us. We're all so proud of you." *Talisman, talisman, talisman.* I rolled the word around my brain and slipped the shark's tooth into my Ziploc baggie of pens and pencils I took with me to college.

• • •

My introductory English professor led a discussion on Homer's *The Odyssey* the first week of class, which I thought was a good start, Homer being Greek and all. It had taken me what seemed like approximately two million hours to do the reading. I broke it down into 60-page increments, racing myself to reduce my per-page reading rate with each section. I was seriously hoping for a gold star of completion.

"Now Penelope," the professor began, "uses the loom like some sort of talisman as she waits for Odysseus to return, but what is the counter-symbolism between what is going on in Penelope's home and what Odysseus is facing in the cave with the Cyclops?"

At that moment I very, very much wanted to be transported into a cave with a Cyclops and wild pigs, who would mercifully impale me on a blunt object and throw me into the sea. The fanciest word I had ever heard in my life was just dropped in passing as a part of a conversation. I had no idea how to answer the professor's question. I could barely handle the reading, much less any deep analysis. Yale and I had both made a horrible mistake.

Yale's president had predicted as much. In his speech at our opening convocation he'd warned all students and parents, "You will think at some point that an admission error was made. It was not. We chose you." I wasn't so sure.

Grades at Yale were always written on the back page of the paper: a private conversation between the student and the grader, whose job it was to make the student into a clearer thinker and writer. That first paper I got back, on *The Odyssey*, had a jarring grade on the last page, along with the comment, "You write like a public school kid." *Guilty as charged.* I was sure that I'd be found out as a fraud for being there, sure that I'd fail out. I studied like a fiend, signed up for every writing intensive seminar and tutorial I could, and exploited my roommate Eva's editorial skills.

Each Sunday night I called my mom and wept, "I can't do this. Everyone else has read more. They talk differently."

"*Everyone's* read more?"

"Well, I guess not everyone."

"Find the other ones who look around the room the way you do."

Sometimes, I just wanted a break, "Mama, I want to come home for the weekend."

"I know, honey. But we can't afford that. This is part of the cost of going away."

"I'm just so tired."

"I know."

Most weeks, at the end of the call, when there was nothing left to say, but I was still so overwhelmed, my mom would suggest, "How about a prayer?" She'd pray with me over the phone for my professors and tutors and roommates and nascent friendships…and for sleep.

We prayed. I studied, and I began to host board game parties in my ever-ugly dorm room. I hosted board game parties because that's what my family did when we got together. We played games. Also, I figured that maybe I could build up good graces should I be exposed for who I really was and expelled. *Kat? Kat who? Oh, that chick who hosted sort of weird pre-bars with Trivial Pursuit. She was nice enough.*

They came. They played. They conquered, and quickly. I had never before seen a full game of Trivial Pursuit completed with all the rules observed in under an hour. I don't think I answered a single question on the board. I just got to be surrounded by people I had begun to love and watch the group cohere amongst itself. Freshman became graduates. Dorm mates became the sort of lifelong friends you get from going through a tough experience together. We're friends from when we were scared of being found out and kicked out and sent back to the communities that had worked so hard to launch us.

A few of us, including my friend Vid, moved from that dorm only an architectural mother could love to Washington, D.C. Vid was attending law school. We'd both spent our childhoods moving and constantly being new, so we navigated that new city together with the same determined intensity—its ins and outs and unspoken rules. We attended each other's parties (his Bar Review; my Orphan Easter celebrations) even though neither of us was the target audience, because we cared about the host.

Vid moved out to San Francisco the same year I began divinity school in Connecticut. Each time we talked, he bid me to come and join him. "You'd love the Bay Area," he promised. "Everyone's from somewhere else, like in D.C., but much more chill. I'm staying." During those years on opposite coasts he began dating an Indian woman, and things moved quickly. I met her for the first time at their wedding—a grand affair complete with drum parades and fire ceremonies—mere days after I'd arrived in California.

Over the course of my six months in California I've met her again several times, but I still don't know her well. I know that she is adorable—a lawyer *and* a dancer, killer smile, always brings a hostess gift and remembers birthdays (which I am horrible at), and has thick, black, shiny hair that never sticks straight out from her head like my unfortunate combination of Einstein and Buckwheat stuck in a humidity chamber. Beyond that, I assume that anyone my friend has chosen is wonderful.

In an attempt to feel at home in Northern California, I have people over to play games.

The snacks are out. The drinks are flowing. We are about 45 minutes into a death match of Trivial Pursuit, an hour and a half into the party. The quiet folks are killing, as they always do. The doorbell rings, and my friend from the dorm, Vid, and his new wife are on the front stoop. She has brought a plate of cookies. Vid shrugs out of his raincoat and leans in to give a greeting hug. He whispers, "She doesn't do games."

This is going to be a hard one. Many of my friends are straight men. This means two things. First, it means that we have rejected one another as romantic partners, sometimes in awkward moments, but more often than not it never came to a public declaration or rejection. We just mutually didn't pursue those lines of conversation. Second, when the guys choose a romantic partner, she becomes my primary point of contact and relationship with the couple. Call me old-fashioned, but I say I'm just a pragmatist. Any time you have a friendship in which there could be sexual tension, it makes sense to me to insulate against that. It doesn't mean that sexual tension ever disappears, no more in friendships than in the workplace, but we set up barriers for ourselves so as not to act on the tensions that rise and fall. I love my male friends, and I want to continue to be friends with them. We rejected each other for good reasons, and I don't want to be even a tangential cause for stress in their romantic relationships.

Cultivating a friendship with the woman my male friend has chosen makes sense, but the process is much easier when she is mostly my doppelganger: she's me, but Nordic/atheist/math-oriented. Vid's wife doesn't do games, which is so much a part of who I am. Somehow, and I know this sounds ridiculous and narcissistic, but somehow it seems like a rejection of me. I moved to California in part because of Vid, and now it turns out that his wife will be a tough transfer of friendship. What else doesn't she do? Does she not vote? Is she not an organ donor?

I have a very refined, specific, panic response in moments like these that I refer to as the Bank Teller Canister. It only happens when I am in the midst of people I care about, in a time and place when I should be in my social groove. It's happened to me at friends' weddings and at New Year's parties and at Fourth of July cookouts. It has happened to me attending church events and leading worship. The common denominator is that I'm someplace where I expect to be having a great time with great people I know.

Then, I'll make a joke that flops, or suggest an activity no one else wants to do, or try to launch a church initiative, or the conversation moves on its own in a direction I can't quite seem to connect to, and a Plexiglas wall descends between me and the people I was just talking to.

It is the absolute worst, most condemning version of loneliness I know. In these moments, loneliness arrives like a quarantine vessel, and I am Bubble Girl, alone and isolated in the midst of everyone. I feel like I am enclosed in one of those plastic bank teller canisters that move through the vacuum tubes at the drive-up windows.

I should be on my A-game of integration and inclusion, and instead I'm alone in the crowd. I reframe my entire life as always being an outsider, and project forward into a future of remaining outside. I will never be at home anywhere, which is a normal fear in the period of being new, but projecting forward isn't helpful. No matter where I move, I'll always be an outsider. The situation has all the makings of *la dolce vita*, and yet, the very things that should alleviate loneliness—being with people I love, doing things I love—have not kept loneliness at bay. I cannot trigger these responses, and greater life stressors don't bring them on. They just happen.

That my sense of loneliness in the midst of people I love, and who love me, will always be part of my life feels like multi-layered condemnation. At a practical, secular level, I'm a doomed loner. But also, Christianity is based on the notion of community—community on earth and community within Godself—so I'm a fraud as a Christian too.

When asked which commandment is the greatest, Jesus replies: the love of God and neighbor. Christians live out our love of God through our love for our fellow humans. This concept goes back to the very earliest Christian communities in the book of Acts. These Christians were known to share their goods with one another and live out a communal life. As a clergy person, part of my job will be to foster the growth of human communities on earth, to encourage them to support one another as we try to serve our communal God. Lord knows I preach and teach about this stuff—but how can I, if I don't feel it or believe it myself?

Plus, the very knowledge of God in Godself is always communal in Christianity. God is always the Trinity. The Divine is always a team. "God" as a title or method of address is always shorthand for Father, Son, and Holy Spirit—or Creator, Redeemer, and Sustainer. God is an abbreviated title. It's like the movie *Precious based on the novel "Push" by Sapphire*, which becomes known in common parlance as just *Precious*. Or think of the plethora of texting/IM abbreviations (e.g., prolly, FWIW, LOL, OMG). Unless otherwise specified, "God" always means "Trinity" in Christianity.

Granted, Christianity within itself somewhat disagrees on exactly what the Trinity means, but both sides of the debate have always agreed that God is Trinity. Early Christian thinkers in Cappadocia* set the course for Eastern Orthodox interpretation of the Trinity. The Cappadocians began with the idea that God was three beings (*hypostaes*) and one essence (*ousia*). The emphasis was on the three interactive beings, like a dance party with all three beings dancing to the same music.

In the Latin-speaking West, Augustine interpreted the Trinity as one substance (*substantia*) and three…three *personae*. *Personae* is usually translated into English as three persons, but the derivation of the word is actually the masks worn in Greek and Roman plays that actors would rotate when they were playing multiple characters in the same show. The Trinity in the West became understood as one substance and three roles. The unity

---

* Northern Turkey.

of the substance was more heavily emphasized than the three masks the one God may wear. However, even if we can't always agree internally on just what we meant by the Trinity, Christianity holds that, no matter what, God in Godself is a group of three.

Community is big in Christianity. Really, really big. So suffice it to say that when the Plexiglas tube of loneliness encases me in the midst of a party at which I know everyone (because it's *my party*), I feel like a warped antisocial freak and a Christian hypocrite.

At these moments I really, really want the Jesus portrayed in John's gospel—because, for my money, he's the only version of Jesus that seems really lonely even in the midst of his friends.* Toward the end of the gospel, there's a story about Jesus being at a dinner party with his pals.** Jesus is trying to explain something about himself and his game plan for the future, and he just isn't connecting with his gumbas. No one, not Philip or Peter, no one picks up what Jesus is putting down. At one point Philip tries to speak on behalf of the rest of the friends and ask for a point of clarification, which really frustrates Jesus. Even the one friend who Jesus loves more than all the rest, who is such a close friend that some translations say he's resting his head on Jesus' chest;*** even this friend doesn't throw Jesus a bone.

Jesus endears himself to me in these authentic, awkward moments because maybe Jesus knows what it's like to be me.**** Maybe I'm not so alone in this experience of life. Maybe part of being human was that Jesus also had the sense I do—that my true identity and belonging is stuck in another zip code that I can never quite seem to find, or, as the psalmist writes in Psalm 119, "I am a stranger here on earth." I don't quite belong here—and maybe never will.

At that dinner party, John writes that Jesus repeated a phrase over and over again: "I came from the Father and have come into the world; again, I am leaving the world and am going to the Father." It's almost like Jesus is reminding himself of who he is: *I'm part of something bigger. There is a bigger plan. I'm part of a unity of love.*

---

* John alone has Jesus change his followers' titles from disciples to friends (chapter 15), whereas in the other gospels, Peter and the gang are always disciples (students) or apostles (messengers).
** The other gospels have the dinner party but tell the story differently.
*** There have always been discussions on the nature of Jesus' relationship with this friend. For the purposes of this essay, I'm assuming that they're just friends and that Jesus was very, very secure. He lounges about with men. They've just washed feet. It was like a dude's locker room. Chalk it up to cultural difference the same way women hold hands walking down the street in France. I digress.
**** The inverse doesn't follow—that I know what it's like to be God, but John's Jesus could maybe know what it's like to be me.

Then Jesus tells his followers that someone/thing is to come after him, and that it is also part of the plan. The *parakletos*,* Jesus tells his friends at the party, will "bring to remembrance all I've said to you" and "not leave you orphaned." *Parakletos* translates directly as "one called alongside," and has been translated into modern language as the Spirit of Remembering or the Spirit of Reminding or, most commonly, the Holy Spirit. Jesus is part of some larger effort, and there will be some Spirit that will come to remind his friends who Jesus was.

I don't claim to understand how God works within Godself and how you can have fully three things and one thing at the same time without doing fractions. What I do get, though, is the irony** that, when Jesus is most alone toward the end of the gospel of John, he reveals himself to be part of a larger, collective whole. And when I am feeling most alone and isolated, God reveals Godself to me as Trinity too. When I am at my absolute loneliest among people, if I can ward off the instinct to consume an entire platter of appetizers and thereby drown my woes in a self-induced carb Quaalude fog, sometimes I can hear a voice that sounds something like mine—but warmer—saying, "I know you're sad. I know you're scared. There was a before. There will be an after. Stay at the party."

That voice, I have decided, is my experience of the *parakletos*. It is probably around all the time, but I am open to being reminded that I am connected to something bigger when I feel the most alone or most afraid of remaining alone.

Blink.

These experiences are fast—in and out of a wormhole in milliseconds. The intensity, though, is like tasting baker's extract. To the casual observer, nothing has taken place. The coats are draped over my left arm, and in my right hand I'm holding the plate of cookies. No time has actually passed, and the evening is not derailed. I am still at the party, still have just had the experience of being isolated, and yet I am somehow integrated into something immeasurably greater than my personhood. The reassurance that I'm seen and affirmed and not alone allows me to do what the voice instructs—to stay at the party. With the Holy Trinity, I am a bit less fraudulent, a bit less alone, a bit more integrated.

I put the cookies on the table, get Vid and his wife drinks, and return to the game. We laugh. We play. Vid's wife even answers a few questions,

---

* Pear-uh-clee-tos. My divinity school's (surprisingly competitive) soccer team was called the Pair a Cleats. *Groan.*
** And not in the Alanis Morissette sense of the word.

shyly, by night's end. The party is a great success; each of us spending time together and becoming part of something bigger than ourselves.

Discussion Questions:

- Have you ever felt isolated in the middle of a crowd, even a crowd of friends? Have you ever felt that way at church or with a group of Christians?
- When you think of the word *God*, do you think of the Trinity?
- Is there one *personae* (Father, Son, Holy Spirit) of the Trinity that you default to when you imagine or communicate with God?
- How does the math work that God is three and one at once?
- Is it more important to you that God be three, or that God be one?

9

Wolf Blitzer at
a Cocktail Party
Being Known

There are things I still miss about being a community development lobbyist in D.C. Certain aspects of it I've been able to recreate in other ways—the curriculum-building piece of trying to break down complex policy issues into the smallest possible bites, in order to explain the impact that draft legislation would have in any one district; the number-crunching of federal budget documents; the building of coalitions of groups with common interests; and the building of relationships. No matter where you are and what you do, relationship building is the same: it's finding a point of common interest and growing to care about the other person.

But what was unique and heady and almost intoxicating, during that time in D.C., was the sense of something always being at stake. We were working for the shelter of homeless New Yorkers, the ability of Denver-ites to have safe roads, the job training of dropouts in San Jose. To be trusted with the well-being of others is compelling and electrifying. I miss the adrenaline drip of importance.

I never, though, grew to love the booze-and-schmooze receptions that are part of building relationships and coalitions in D.C. On the positive side, these evening receptions were the chance to put names with faces and connect a real, breathing human with someone you'd only known by e-mail. There is no substitute for incarnate relationships. And they were the best places to get the eyes and ears of incredibly busy Capitol Hill staffers. While I was working on community development issues, their portfolios would include not only community development but also banking reform and pensions and a whole host of other topics. Face time was key to getting staffers to focus on my issues.

For me, though, the receptions were always work. Not so for Vid, my college friend who loved networking receptions so much that he'd sometimes tag along with me as a study break while he was in law school in D.C. Presumably there are also people who like spinal tap procedures and intricate tax forms.

Not that I was a wallflower. I tend to think that I looked like a brunette Tinkerbell, flitting from key person to person, getting to know them—and genuinely so. From the moment I grabbed my stick-on nametag at the door and did a visual inventory of the room, I was off to the races, working the crowd. But I always envied a bit the Capitol Hill staffers who got to stand in one place while others approached them.

Being clergy at a church coffee hour is a little bit like being a Capitol Hill staffer. You stand still, and people want to talk to you—and not just talk to you, but to share deeply important, personal matters about their lives; the sort of things you only share with your closest friends or therapist or clergy person. When I interned at a parish in central Connecticut for a few years, I'd only have to say, "So how was your week?" and a torrent of fragility would pour out. Having that experience is its own sort of ego boost.

But at church coffee hour here in California, I'm not clergy. I'm just a new member who doesn't really know anybody. I am standing to the side one Sunday, eyeing the children who run and scream while adults of a certain age wince because their hearing aids can't block out the kids. Haggard young parents try to engage in adult conversation with one another for a few precious moments. Matriarchs and patriarchs hold court in their usual spots.

Then the "Issue Hawk" descends on me. God bless the Issue Hawks. These people get things done. Thanks to them, refugees' apartments get set up, foster children have Christmas presents, blood banks are replenished, and aid packages are sent throughout the developing world. Several thumbs are broken and arms twisted in the process, but so be it. And God bless this Issue Hawk for having no discretion in who she attacks, even *moi*.

"Is your cup empty?" she demands, multi-colored garbage bags tied to her belt loops.

I look into the weak, milky brew that I've been nursing, which has turned cold. "Nope, I'm still working on it."

"Well, finish it up then."

"Will do!" I answer.

But then she doesn't leave. "I'll wait," she says, hands on her hips, bags flapping like the deflated ends of a crusader cape. Confused about what I could have done wrong, I down the remnants in one gulp and hold the empty cup up in a "Cheers!" motion.

"Turn your cup over. See that emblem there? All compostable. Made from corn. Goes here in the brown bag. Brown for compost. Anything with that emblem goes in the brown bag. Coffee grounds, tea bags, and all the cups and plates with that emblem."

"Well, great. That'll be easy to remember. Brown for anything that can be turned back into dirt. Got it."

She shakes her head. "You're exactly why I voted against brown bags for compost. The colors are going to reinforce ignorance. Compost is not the same thing as dirt."

I really can't win on this one. "Okay, I'll remember brown for compost like coffee grounds."

"Kat, I've put some white papers about this issue on the church website under the Eden Commission, and I think that it would be a good thing for you to read them. I think that you're really at the stage of gaining awareness." I appreciate an unsolicited diagnosis of my shortcomings. "Do you have a composting system at home right now?" she asks.

"I don't, but I live in an apartment and don't have a yard..."

"A low-odor worm system is perfect for you. Yep, just about the size of two shoeboxes. You can put it anywhere you want—under your sink, on the counter—and just feed the worms your scraps, and you'll get really beautiful compost as they process everything. And even if you can't use it, quality compost is an excellent gift."

I try for a moment to picture myself at Christmas, handing out festive gift bags of home-harvest worm compost. She's on to the next victim by the time I return to the present. And I am back to having to find someone to talk to.

The upside of being anonymous is that no one at the church in California cares whether I'm there or not, and no one makes comments about how much I eat or don't eat, or whether I'm having a bad hair day (all of which are common when I'm serving as clergy). But I miss being known and recognized and having a public role where people want to talk to me.

The words of the woman from the bishop's office in Connecticut come back to me: that the ordaining commission wants me to explore my baptismal covenant and really think about what it means to live out my Christian faith without being clergy.

But, darn it, I don't want to be me. I want to be Wolf Blitzer.* The emerging Asian tech boom brought my family to Hong Kong in the late 1980s/early 1990s for my dad's job. The first Gulf War brought Wolf Blitzer into our living room via CNN on satellite at least once a day.

One of Wolf's main contributions to my childhood was that he was a connection to Western media. Aside from Wolf, our pre-Internet screen options were limited to bootleg videos from Bangkok. These were just like being in a real movie theater—shadows of peoples' heads blocking parts of the screen, sneezing and laughter drowning out key lines in the plot—except the bootlegs included the added benefit of vertigo because they were made by people taking camcorders into movie theaters and resting them on their laps.

Hong Kong International School offered students Western entertainment in the form of visiting "world tours" by Christian entertainment troupes with positive, uplifting messages. A Seventies-era building of large wooden beams served as our church on Sundays, and as the school chapel/stage during the rest of the week. Onto the stage came the Up with People songster and a whimsical comedy troupe, who showed that you could have fun while sober, and a serious theater ministry of dramatic enactments of appropriate touch.

I clapped wildly for these performances, mostly because my mother had taught us that artists are paid in applause, and I could tell that these folks might not have such a bright future ahead of them. Best to seed their applause chests early so that they'd have something to live on.

I also clapped because of who they weren't, namely the Americans affiliated with the school who "discovered" their true ministries and callings in Hong Kong, freed from the shackles of American competition. I am thinking in particular of the rather zaftig woman with unfortunate teeth whose self-discerned gift was Christian clowning. She would don a polka dot polyester suit and grease paint, and would mime the words to Vatican II-era praise songs, ending in a series of whirling dervish turns lasting whatever length of time (often much longer than the song) necessary to end by raising a bleeding-heart-of-Jesus balloon sculpture in triumph.

*

Up with People also saved us from the director music, who enforced musical enrichment in the form of organ recitals on the lesser works of Bach all fourth and fifth graders. There's a reason that lesser works are lesser works.

Ellen and me on the first day of school, Hong Kong, 1990

Hong Kong International School was a missionary outpost of the Lutheran Church Missouri Synod, and that middle school chapel/Sunday worship space served as the nexus of our lives as American expatriates. The church staff and most of the teachers and school administrators were there as missionaries, and they provided the structure of life for the expatriate families. We lived and learned and worshiped and worked together nearly every day of the week. The church fellowship hall always had a certain bouquet of sweat, because during the week it was the school gymnastics room, complete with pommel horses and balance beams. Our Sunday school rooms were weekday classrooms and also the space where we would make care packages for the soldiers who'd stop by on their way to Kuwait.

When the bomb threats started against the school, I wasn't too upset. As an American, it wasn't unique to be a negative target in Hong Kong. Local residents would spit at me and yell "*Guilo!*" which meant "round-eyed devil." Hong Kong residents spit a lot though. It wasn't personal.

But this was different. When these calls started, we practiced duck-and-cover drills, such as how to slide below the window level of the school bus in case shots were fired through the windows. Soon the threats and drills became normal. We would hope for bomb threats on math test days. Boys staged their own chemical warfare by releasing silent but deadly farts when we were all crouched down on the school bus, with the windows closed.*

What I didn't realize at the time was that the American Consulate in Hong Kong took these bomb threats extremely seriously. Hong Kong was

---

* Average annual temperature 86ºF and over 50% humidity.

a major, cosmopolitan port where poor workers came from all over Asia—China, the Philippines, Indonesia—for work. The many cultures slammed against one another made Hong Kong a fascinating place to be a child, but it also became a microcosm for the spread of Western Capitalism, in which poor workers from across Asia worked in service to Western companies and expatriates. Racial-cultural tensions could be raw in Hong Kong, and my school was the symbolic heart of the ugly American. My parents and their friends went through extensive evacuation drills, and the school had an emergency phone tree set up by neighborhood so that someone in each neighborhood was on-call every day and knew where that day's emergency evacuation site was.

The first bomb threats were unsophisticated crank calls. A man would call the school office and say something to the effect of "Is this American school?" "Bomb you." *Oh, bomb you too.* But as a precaution, all of the kids filed out of the building and onto the beach to sing "Michael Row Your Boat Ashore" until the school could be checked for explosives. We were told not to wear our red, white, and blue uniforms lest we broadcast that we were Americans. I'm not sure it was only the school uniforms that gave us away. (See comment above on being a "round-eyed devil.")

Then came the call from a self-possessed Western-sounding female who phoned the school office to inform them that a bomb had been planted under the middle school chapel/stage. Her knowledge of the place and specificity were taken seriously. We were shuttled quickly home, where we huddled around our only source of information, Wolf Blitzer, to hear the latest on the war.

During the first Gulf War, American government officials coined the term "the CNN Effect" to describe the impact of the 24-hour news cycle on how official decisions started to be made in response to constant media surveillance. CNN was broadcasting footage of the war from across the Middle East as it was happening, and government officials had less time to make decisions. But as an American child abroad, the CNN Effect was one of comfort and identity. Any hour of the day in Hong Kong, Wolf Blitzer would give me the straight scoop on what was happening between President Bush and his swarthy opponent Hussein. I was an American, and America was at war, and by virtue of being an American, I was at risk. But Wolf's very presence explaining things reassured me that things would be okay.

In the way that things are often less dramatic than they first appear, the bomb call about the middle school was made by an American student who called from a pay phone in the lobby of the school itself. We were our own worst enemy.

• • •

Fifteen years later, I was a lobbyist attending a reception at the Time Warner Building in New York City during the 2004 Republican National Convention. I spent most of the night squinting and trying surreptitiously to look down at a bulging stack of mini index cards on a key ring in my hand. Each card had a photo of a Republican member of Congress, copied from the Congressional directory, on the front, and his or her connection to any issues I was working on for my clients on the back.

The point in going to such events as a lobbyist is to get face time with elected officials on behalf of your issue. Mine was affordable housing in New York City. The problem is that elected officials look nothing like their Glamour Shots in the Congressional Directory, and there are about 267 Republican members of Congress at any one time, not to mention the secretaries and under-secretaries of the federal agencies. I was squinting as people walked around, trying to see if twenty pounds, ten years, and a good toupee ago they might have been one of the people on my index cards.

I was scanning the room, mid-squint, a skewer of coconut shrimp on a stick in my left hand and index cards in my right, when there he was, the silver fox himself, Wolf Blitzer. I would know him anywhere. *Hello, old friend.* My face brightened into a smile. I started to walk toward him.

He looked in my direction. I tried to catch his eye, angling my neck into his line of vision and quickened my step, but he looked right past me, and on to someone that he recognized. I was just some anonymous woman in a little black dress, holding a skewer of coconut shrimp and trying desperately to connect. He didn't know me at all. He was the reception rock star. I was the fan.

So I am mortified when I realize that I want to be Wolf at the church coffee hour—the person sought out. I want people to want to talk to me, to feel an intimacy with me and want to connect.

Or, maybe, what I really want is to be known.

There's a coming-of-age rite in the Episcopal Church known as Rite 13,* which follows two years of adolescents defining their faith for themselves. It's an invitation for tweens to ask the questions their hearts and minds are beginning to ponder.

As part of the ceremony the congregation and tweens read a modified translation of Psalm 139 responsively. Up front are a bunch of thirteen year olds in the throes of orthodontia torture. The rest of the congregation

---

* It's sort of like confirmation rites.

sit safely in their seats. Back and forth, we affirm that the tweens and we
are good, and created in God's image, and intimately known to God.

Tweens:
LORD, you have searched me out and known me;
you know my sitting down and my rising up;
you discern my thoughts from afar.
If I take the wings of the morning
and dwell in the uttermost part of the sea,
Even there your hand will lead me
and your right hand hold me fast.

Congregation:
Your works are wonderful, and I know it well.

Tweens:
For you yourself created my inmost parts;
you knit me together in my mother's womb.
I will thank you because I am marvelously made;
your works are wonderful, and I know it well.

Congregation:
Your works are wonderful, and I know it well.

Tweens:
My body was not hidden from you,
while I was being made in secret
and woven in the depths of the earth.
Your eyes beheld my limbs, yet unfinished in the womb;
all of them were written in your book;
they were fashioned day by day,
when as yet there were none of them.

Congregation:
Your works are wonderful, and I know it well.

Tweens:
Search me out, O God, and know my heart;
try me and know my restless thoughts.
Look well whether there be any wickedness in me
and lead me in the way that is everlasting.

Congregation:
Your works are wonderful, and I know it well.[15]

Each time we do the ceremony, I am reminded that the example of God's work that I know best, me, is wonderful, as are the fantastic tweens. I long to be known and named, just like the psalmist does. God's work we know best—ourselves—is wonderful.

In California I am far from known, and I'd like someone else to do the legwork of building the relationships, thank you very much.

I look around at coffee hour and what I see are a bunch of people, each holding a coffee cup or a piece of pastry in one hand. Their clothes are nondescript. Their eyes scan for someone to talk to. Necks crane like baby birds. Each of us is just trying to connect. Who am I, if I am not clergy? I am a Christian, a child of God, trying to feel integrated in this world. And so it begins:

"How was your week?"

Discussion Questions:

- What does it mean to be known by others or by God?
- How is being known different from being the center of attention?
- Have you ever been the enemy because of how you looked or who you were?
- Do you have a memory of a teenage coming-of-age ritual?

10

Tax Fraud and My Little Pony

Doing Ministry

Betsy's cough sounds like an asthmatic seal barking for a mate, long after all the prospects have swum away. It's mournful and low and choppy and just on the brink of asphyxiation. She suffers from the aftereffects of whooping cough. If we were on the Oregon Trail, we would have dumped her body in Missouri and picked up slabs of bacon and musket ammo in the amount of her body weight. Instead, we are in her living room in Silicon Valley, surrounded by DVD cases and boxes of tissues. Betsy's strawberry blond hair shudders with each cough. Her fair cheeks flush. I focus on filling in a My Little Pony coloring book page to give her some privacy in her consumptive fit. She doesn't like to be watched. But she keeps coughing and coughing, so I stare out the window at the (February) spring blossoms and at the wedding pictures on her mantle. Betsy and her wife Jen had a shotgun wedding of sorts—expedited by Proposition 8.* All three of us are about the same age and height, though Jen is as olive-skinned and strappingly healthy as Betsy is fair and frail. At a barbeque Jen picks up a Frisbee, while Betsy stirs iced tea. We have arrived at this scene because I am a friend of both women, and also, I oversee human resources for the nonprofit where Betsy and I both work, and she is one of my humans.

---

* In May 2008 the California Supreme Court ruled that marriage between two adults was a constitutional right under the state constitution. In November 2008, the California voters passed a constitutional amendment defining marriage as between opposite sex adults only.

Back in the fall, I had called my sister Margo to bemoan my state of not being clergy at coffee hour and not being swept into international missionary work. I could sense her giving me a (nearly) audible eye roll. Then she said (with no compassion at all), "Kathryn, you just have to change your understanding of who you consider your church to be. You go to your office every single day. Minister to them. Be their pastor."

"But I work as an entry-level fundraising associate. I write grant proposals."

My argument didn't even deserve a response. Margo just waited silently until I realized the insanity of what I'd just said—that I couldn't do ministry where I was. Sometimes I hate having a sister who's brilliant in her ability to synthesize, eleven years younger, and a blatant Evangelical.

So I engaged in the magic prayer formula: lifting up a question to God, working my butt off to do my part, and then trying to remain vigilant for surprise answers to the prayer. The prayer I prayed for myself and asked my small group friends to pray on my behalf was something like, "God, give me eyes to see how I can minister to the people around me." My part of the prayer work began with crawling around in the attic of the converted auto-repair garage that now housed the nonprofit where I worked. I dragged down some lamps, an old TV tray table, and box labeled "Birthday" filled with candles. In a corner of my office, the candles went atop the rickety TV dinner table for ambience beside an dingy Ikea armchair that had been a catch-all of old pamphlets. *Voila* —a pastoral care and counseling corner. Lucy of the Peanuts comic strip was open for business. *Tell me your woes, and I will listen with my chaplaincy nonanxious presence.*

I waited a long time to be surprised, and nothing happened. My coworkers would sometimes come in and sit on the chair for the novelty of it. Betsy and I were often the only people in the office early in the morning, so she'd come in with her mug of tea, and we'd chat before the phones started ringing. We were the same age and read the same books and listened to the same radio programs. We began to become friends during those mornings. Aside from that half hour each day, though, the chair stood empty. I felt like a doofus—a doofus learning more and more about fundraising, but a doofus nonetheless.

A few months later, though, our bookkeeper quit, and the organization's director asked if I would like to take on the bookkeeping and human resources in addition to fundraising work.* The last time I took

---

* Those of you schooled in best practices will note that the person who does fundraising (soliciting cash) is never supposed to be the person keeping the books (counting the cash). You would be right. See above on being a teeny-tiny nonprofit operating out of a garage. This is not an excuse but rather a statement of fact.

math was my junior year of high school, which is also, coincidentally, the last time I balanced my checkbook down to the penny. But I knew enough math to know that my loan payments from seminary, my therapy bills, and the costs of living in the Bay Area were more than I could handle on my current salary just doing the fundraising work. So, sure, I'd do the finances.

The old bookkeeper handed over a *Basic Principles of Accounting* textbook, a binder of state labor regulations, and her cell phone number. I took a three-day training on how to use our accounting software, signed up for some one-hour webinars on California labor laws, and before I could say "No thanks, Jesus. This isn't what I had in mind," I was the completely ill-equipped Director of Finance, Resources, and Donor Relations.

I held fast to the Blanche DuBois management model in those first months, completely relying upon the kindness of strangers. People I had never met before were insanely good to me. There was the team of outside, private auditors who, along with my predecessor on speed dial, helped me to close the previous year's books. Everyone makes mistakes in a new job, but when you make them as the director of finance it's called fraud, and it's illegal. This was very scary.

Then there was the uptight human resources consultant who stopped in the middle of his sales pitch to put the Occupational Safety and Health Administration workplace safety posters in our break area in alignment and compliance because he "just couldn't stand the mess." His neurosis kept us from getting fined.

And then there was Fred, dear Fred, the beleaguered IRS agent who appeared in our office unannounced to inform me that he was just getting around to some cold cases, and our organization had an outstanding violation from a decade earlier. There I was, director of finance, and there he was, the IRS, the one thing I was working my hiney off to avoid. I reverted back to the last time I had been quite so panicked in a professional setting: when I was the chaplain on call at an inner-city trauma unit and two warring gangs came into the emergency room. I put into place what I'd learned that summer in the ER. I went completely chaplain on Fred's ass.

I showed him to the Ikea chair and offered him tea. Then I engaged in reflective listening, which basically involved me saying back to him as a question exactly what he'd just said as a statement, as in, "Wow, so what I'm hearing is that you need some documentation from our checking account from ten years ago, is that right? Gosh, tell me more." He did, God bless him. He told me exactly the documentation he needed and in what format and what to say in the cover letter and which office to send it to. Fred the IRS agent ministered to me so, so very much.

Keeping in line with the state and federal finance and labor regulations was my external challenge. I was given the internal task of "communicating our austerity budget" to the staff, which meant informing the staff that no one was getting a raise; that we'd have to cut shared costs; and that each department's expenditures were getting slashed. Adding insult to injury, the budgeting process had been pretty opaque before, so none of the managers knew what their expenditures had been in the past or how things were allocated. Super.

As to whether I succeeded or failed, you'd have to ask my colleagues, but what I tried to do was approach the task as ministry by asking myself, "What would be the most loving and pastoral way to handle this with my colleagues?" I opened up the financial records and walked through what each category meant with each manager and gave them access to all past and current expenses. That way they could see exactly what they had spent before and were spending in the present in order to figure out how to cut. Each manager took a different austerity approach. One put off staff hiring. Another shook down a print shop in town to do her promotional materials at a discount. A third made client appreciation gifts from scratch instead of purchasing them. The entire staff decided which shared expenses to cut (print newspapers) and which to retain (coffee). Budgeting became a very public, very shared project. The money and the time was ours, together, and so were the solutions.

I prayed for my coworkers each morning as I swam laps at the community pool, going around the office cubicle by cubicle in my head. I lifted up their work and lives and families. Often I asked God to help me learn how best to encourage the young woman who reported to me, how managing might become part of my ministry so that I could guide her in a way that affirmed her gifts and made her most ready for her future. With each lap and with each day, so incrementally that I almost didn't realize that it was happening, I gorged on fewer midnight quesadillas drenched in tears and fantasized less about decamping to the Caribbean. My life was becoming enmeshed with others'.

All that winter and spring Betsy battled the cough that stayed around years after her contagion left. She could do much of her work as a program assistant remotely, which was good because her coughing fits silenced the office—as in drowning out anyone's attempt at conversation as the coughs and gasps ricocheted off the walls. If Betsy hadn't been so conscientious— in trying to step outside to cough and being obviously embarrassed and in banking her lunch hours to go to one specialist after another and assuring us that she wasn't contagious—it might have created a problem in office morale. Betsy tried so hard to manage her chronic condition, and Silicon

Valley is so wired that even a small nonprofit housed in a converted auto garage was fully equipped to have employees work remotely. Often, it was easier for everyone to communicate with Betsy through e-mail while she worked from home than to collaborate in person.

One day, though, Betsy calls me to say that she's home but not working from home. She's taking it as a personal day because her dad is having emergency open-heart surgery, and she just can't concentrate. My job as HR person means that I am supposed to receive this information and enter her personal day into her timesheet. If I want to be really conscientious, I can double-check the provisions of the Family Medical Leave Act to see what her options will be if she needs to take time off to care for her dad in the future. Really, though, I just need to enter in her personal day and keep quiet.

The problem with this course of action is that Betsy is my friend and my congregant. I know that her wife is away on business all week. I know that she is home alone, sick, while her father is being cut open. I cannot get myself to leave HR protocol well enough alone. I ask if I can come by. As soon as she says, "Uhhhh, okay, I guess, but you really don't have to," I am out of the office and on my way to her home because in moments of trauma it is good not to be completely alone. I pick up some coloring books and crayons on the way, thinking it will give her something to do with her hands while she waits. And who doesn't like the regression therapy of coloring books with a box of sharp, new crayons? Answer: *Betsy*. She is totally weirded out by the coloring books, but the visit is good. We sit. She coughs and cries and says aloud to another person how scared and helpless she feels.

In the car driving home, I smirk a bit when it occurs to me that I have done what Margo told me to do: I've made my workplace into my congregation in how I approach my work there. What's more, I just might have begun to live out my baptismal covenant right where I am.

I'm beginning to believe that this is how "call" or "vocation"* happens, that we live into what God has called us to do and be when situations present themselves. I didn't pursue doing nonprofit administration and human resources because there was a distinct voice of God. I needed to pay rent.

There was not, much to my disappointment, a Samuel moment. I have always wanted a Samuel moment. Samuel, in the book of Samuel in the Hebrew Bible, is an adolescent, serving as a lackey to an elderly temple priest named Eli who has begun to lose his eyesight. Late one night while Samuel is drowsily watching the lamp at the Ark of the covenant burn out,

---

* From the Latin *vocatio*, meaning a call or summons.

he hears a voice calling his name, "Samuel, Samuel." So he runs into his mentor Eli's room, saying, "Here I am, for you called me." Eli tells Samuel that he didn't call him and to go back to lamp tending. But the voice keeps calling Samuel, and he keeps going to see what Eli wants. The third time, Eli realizes that it just might be the Lord calling Samuel, so he tells Samuel, "Go, lie down; and if he calls you, you shall say, 'Speak, LORD, for your servant is listening.'" The voice comes again. Samuel responds with Eli's words and goes on to discoverer that he is to be a messenger of God's word, and eventually becomes the transitional leader of the Israelites. How very convenient.

This story must have been part of my school or Sunday school curriculum in fourth grade in Hong Kong. We must have been told that Samuel was about our age and were asked, "What would you do if you heard the voice of the Lord calling your name?" *Easy.* I wouldn't dawdle around like Samuel did. I had my response ready. I have vivid memories of seeing those bright splotches that sometimes pass across ones field of vision and immediately excusing myself to the nearest bathroom, taking a knee, and saying aloud, "Speak, Lord, for your servant is listening." This happened more than once. I have a lot of bathroom tile in my memory, all of it met with silence. You can't blame a girl for trying. There are worse things than offering oneself up as the Israelite leader.

Instead, my experience of call or vocation has been more like Esther's experience in the Hebrew Scriptures. Esther is a young, beautiful, orphaned Jewish woman living in Persia under the protection of her uncle Mordecai. After seven days of nonstop drinking and partying, the king of Persia disposes of his first wife and holds a national "beauty pageant" for her replacement, bringing his favorites into the palace for a year of "cosmetic treatments." Esther's uncle Mordecai knows that he's got a looker on his hands and enters her into the running. The king favors her, and after a full year of cosmetic treatments, she rises to the top as one of the very favorites, passing for Persian all along.

Meanwhile, outside the palace gates, Uncle Mort has made a mess of things. He has refused to bow down before the king because Jews saw it as a violation of their honor to the Lord. They only bowed to the Lord, not to any human. One of the king's henchmen notices Mordecai's irreverence and starts a smear campaign to have all Jews killed. Uncle Mort eventually passes Esther a compelling message: "Do not think that in the king's palace you will escape any more than all the other Jews... Who knows? Perhaps you have come to royal dignity for such a time as this." Esther then gets the king liquored up, and he woozily agrees to her request. She saves her people.

Drunken manipulations, pimping out an orphan, and cosmetic treatments aside, Esther is put into a situation she didn't plan, didn't ask for, and isn't even sure what her role is in all of it. She has an opportunity to recast the situation into something pretty great. She becomes the queen of her people because she can. Interestingly enough, God never speaks or appears as a character in Esther's story at all.

Our calls, our vocations, arise out of the contexts in which we find ourselves—whether chosen or not—and involve our lives' colorful, real cast of characters. Sometimes the voice of Uncle Mort comes right in the midst of a situation, posing a version of "Who knows? Perhaps you have come into this situation for just this reason." That's what happened to me in Margo suggesting that I minister in my workplace.

More often, though in my life, it's only after the fact, only in the retelling of some story that I tease out what just might have been the hand of God leading me into a role and giving me an opportunity in my daily life to do God's work right where I was. Maybe all those things happened for just such a reason as this... The vocation, the call, only comes into focus in the rearview.

Who knows? Perhaps I have become the HR person just so I can be there with Betsy. Maybe I've been given the opportunity to do budgeting so that budgeting can mean something different for all of us in that office. Maybe I had to move to California for some reason I just couldn't see at the start.

As Christians we are called to minister to one another wherever we are, in whatever situation we find ourselves. Luther and others in the Protestant Reformation emphasized the notion of the priesthood of all believers, the idea that each of us is a minister of Christ's church in our daily lives. It's a continual theme in Christianity. Pope Leo I (*aka* Leo the Great) wrote about the priesthood of all Christians in a beautiful fifth-century text: "The sign of the cross makes all those who are born again in Christ kings, and the anointing of the Holy Spirit consecrates them all as priests. As a result, apart from the particular service of our ministry, all spiritual and rational Christians are recognized as members of this royal people and sharers in the priestly office [of Christ]."[16]

We are all ministers, priests, and kings in our lives and work. It's like a modification of Abe Lincoln's famous quote to his sons, "Whatever you are, be a good one." The Christian vocation version is, "Whatever you are, be a holy one." Or, at least, that's what begins to dawn on me as I drive home from Betsy's, that I've just done ministry with her. This is, I think, something of what the woman at the bishop's table was going for in Connecticut with all the "living out the baptismal covenant" bit. And I'm really kind of liking it. That's as far as my brain will let me go right then, though the people I love and trust push me to think further.

"Are you sure," ask my sister Ellen, my mom, Eva, Emily, and many others, "that you want to be ordained? You're happier now than you have been in a long time." I'm not sure at all, less sure than I'd been in a long time. To be ordained literally means to be "set apart," but I'm not sure that I want to be set apart. I quite like being embedded.

Can I imagine myself not being ordained? Sure. But I don't like imagining it. I love the church, and my daydream for myself has been in the church for so long, and others have listened with me, and affirmed it too. Plus, there's the sunken opportunity cost of graduate school and the ordination process.

"I'm as sure as I'm going to be," I answer my loved ones (with the conviction of skim milk). "I may as well go through with it at this point."

My therapist does the head tilt thing he does when pondering: "You could end up being like Paul." The *apostle* Paul? The one who's crabby and prone to self-loathing/self-aggrandizement and offending people in print? I'm on it.

My therapist finishes his point: "He always made his living as a tradesman sewing tents. He worked and built God's kingdom and the church."

"But I've come this far. I am not willing to consider giving up on ordination now." I'm very worked up. He's the umpteenth person to have asked me this, and I am holding onto ordination with my fingernails.

Sure, I can imagine making my living in another way, but I can't imagine not working somehow in the church—because I love that shiny, lumpy, crabapple of an institution. I can't imagine a life in which I wasn't asking questions about God in small groups and from the pulpit, wrestling with ancient texts to see where they resonate now. And I couldn't imagine a life without participating in the sacraments of baptism and community. I couldn't imagine a life outside of the church entirely. But ordination isn't required for participation in any of that, not in my tradition.

"I didn't say not to get ordained." *Oh.* "Just, can you imagine living out your ministry not necessarily working in the church full-time, even if you are ordained? This new job with the nonprofit has let you see your ministry differently."

He's right. My education isn't going to waste. I am using it in how I approach my office. I have purpose and direction and call. I am doing ministry, just not the way I'd thought I would be doing it. I could still do church. The possibilities become endless for being a priest in the world. The only question is how I'll be supporting myself.

Excitedly, I float the idea by one of my Episcopal clergy mentors. She freaks out, visibly shaking her head and hands both and says, "But you would be such a good priest. Why are you abandoning the church?"

"I'm not. I would just live out my call in more than one setting. Plus, I'd be cheaper to hire in the church because I wouldn't be full-time!"

"You have to make a choice, Kat—whether to give your life to the church or not. You can't keep one foot on the shore. You need to pray on what you're being called to, because ordination changes you. What is it that you're afraid of? What's keeping you from making the commitment to being a priest?"

I'm not afraid of making a commitment to God or to the church. I'm just living out my call in multiple settings. I'm getting in touch with ye ole baptismal covenant. At least, that's what I thought I was doing.

I don't say anything to any other clergy. I hide my changing mind.

Discussion Questions:

- The author describes her experiences ministering to her coworkers. Have you ever had an opportunity to do ministry in your school, workplace, or another nonreligious setting? What was it like?
- When you look back over your life and experiences, have there been times when you lived into a call or vocation that you hadn't seen coming?
- Have you heard about the idea of the "priesthood of all believers"? What does this mean to you?
- How do live out your ministry?

11

Smells Like Tater Tots

Being Church

My workplace has some of the hallmarks of a church, but it's not the church, and I have come to love and need that which is uniquely church. My office is a loving community, present to one another in crisis, where I am able to live out my baptismal covenant. The organization seeks to improve peoples' lives. We have meaningful work. We are generous with one another. And I do believe that God is present in the midst of our cat's cradle of relationships with one another: colleague to colleague to client to vendor to donor.

But my colleagues at the nonprofit and I do not gather intentionally to try and figure out what it means to believe that there is something bigger than all of us, that our lives have meaning beyond the reach of our fingertips. That is what it is to be church—a motley crew of folks trying to be convinced that they aren't an accident, that they have a purpose bigger than themselves: to love God and one another and to leave their world better than they found it, even if they've had bumps in the road.

We come together and make church because we weren't intended to be alone, at least not all the time, and we need one another to figure out what we're intended for. We come together to figure out our priorities and how to live with hope in the midst of chaos. People in church use songs and stories and conversations and prayers and soup kitchens and landscaping and lots of disagreements to figure those things out.

What makes church "church" depends on what church you go to. Different Christian traditions have different baseline definitions. Both

Eastern Orthodoxy and Roman Catholicism maintain that what is essential about the church is celebrating the Eucharist with historical continuity and accuracy. Both traditions claim to celebrate the sacrament with the right, proper historical practice.* One can have a good-hearted gathering of Christians, but unless a proper Eucharist takes place, it isn't the church.

The Protestant Reformation** emphasized, among other things, the contemporary nature of the church and the telling of the story of the resurrection in the language of the people. The church was wherever apostles—those tasked with preaching the good news of God's kingdom and Jesus' love—were gathered. The Bible was printed in the vernacular; songs were sung to tunes everyone knew or could sing easily; the Word was to be preached in a way that made Scripture accessible and applicable to the gathered assembly. The Eucharist was the celebration of the Lord's supper and an important aspect of worship, but church was bigger than that aspect of worship. This basic understanding of church continues to hold for both the modern Protestant Evangelical movement and modern mainline churches.

The early twentieth century in the United States witnessed a new church movement, known as Pentecostalism. In religious gatherings amongst largely working-class people in Southern California, church became defined by the Holy Spirit descending in a group setting. The Eucharist was completely outside the realm of what defined church, as were any other trappings of organized religion or the historical church. The true church, to Pentecostals, existed only in gatherings where the Holy Spirit chose to speak.

My own religious history covers all the bases. My dad was raised Greek Orthodox. My mom was Roman Catholic. My mother's grandmother was one of the original members of the Pentecostal movement out west. I was raised Lutheran but am now Episcopalian, and my parents and sisters all attend Evangelical churches. Go figure.

We're a Christian family. But we weren't always—not exactly, not together. I tend to think of church as something I need out of habit because I grew up in a Christian household, but that's only a limitation of memory. When I think back on my family life vis-à-vis Christianity I see:

---

* Eastern Orthodoxy tends to emphasize the words of the Eucharistic text itself as the ancient rite. Roman Catholicism has a slightly different emphasis in the whole event of the Eucharistic mass and the priest celebrating the mass as having specific historical continuity, though the words have changed some throughout time.

** The fifteenth through seventeenth centuries in Western and Northern Europe witness a series of (often violent) upheavals arising from a tinderbox of economic, cultural, and religious clashes that are broadly described as the Protestant Reformation.

- Every birthday we have a tradition of going around the table, holding hands, and praying one-by-one for the person whose birthday it is. We first offer thanks for him or her, and the things that we are grateful for about the person's life and the past year, and ask God's blessing on his/her year ahead. The tradition probably began when we were older, but I remember it going back a long time.
- I once lamented a friend going on a really snazzy beach vacation for spring break. My parents responded by explaining to me that we gave ten percent of our money to people in need because we were Christian, and that meant that sometimes we couldn't go on vacation. I didn't like the situation, but I accepted it, somewhat smugly. We didn't go on vacation because we were just a little bit better people.
- I really wanted to skip the birthday party of a very uncool girl during the "mean girl" era of middle school. My mother asked me, "What would it be in this situation to care for the outcast?" Then I felt like a jerk and went to her party.
- We prayed together before big tests and meetings. Prayer was and is part of how we solved problems and hoped.

But those snapshots look backwards through the kaleidoscope. They're not where we began.

Both of my parents grew up in large ethnic enclaves in Chicago. My mom came from an Irish Catholic family, and my Dad grew up Greek Orthodox. Both of their religious traditions, Catholicism and Orthodoxy, claim to be the "One, True Church," relatively unchanged since the time of Christ. So, for either of my parents to leave their denomination was tantamount to leaving the church altogether. Neither felt comfortable in the other's church culture, and neither was willing to be subsumed to the other person's dominance. Their stances were so extreme that they subjected all of their wedding guests to two complete ceremonies—a full Catholic Mass *and* a Greek Orthodox ceremony across town.

Those four hours of non-stop liturgy held them for a while, and they stopped going to church altogether. For young couples to avoid religious practice is very common. Some years into the church-free marriage, I was born, followed three years later by Ellen. Both baby girls were baptized Catholic in private family ceremonies, well-documented through photos and VHS recordings. Again, very common for parents to want babies initiated into the faith community even when they themselves aren't practicing.

But my mother loved church, or, rather, she loved her high school experience of church at an uber-leftist Franciscan* high school run by and for women. By college, she had stopped going, but her formative years took place among women on fire for justice. They marched. They body blocked. They read George Bernard Shaw and Nietzsche. Being Catholic meant working for justice with your mind and heart and other women.

She wanted that for her daughters. So she began taking my squirmy preschool self with her as she church-shopped. Dad stayed home with baby Ellen.

I hesitate to tell you this next story because it's too precious and too prescient for reality and it makes what happened afterward sound far too political. But here goes. On one such shopping trip she was narrating what was happening up front during the Eucharist in an attempt to keep me quiet.

"Where are the girls?" I asked.

"Oh, girls aren't allowed up front in this church."

"Are they allowed up front in other churches?"

"Yes."

"Then why are we here?"

Why did she give me that opening, "in this church"? Didn't she know that a four-year-old would hear that loophole and tear it wide open? Why didn't she just say men are priests?

Some weeks later she was at a League of Women Voters meeting, as she often was at that time, working on something related to the Equal Rights Amendment. One of the other women there was a Protestant clergyman's wife and asked my mother, "I mean this in all seriousness; how do you stay with the Catholic church when working on women's issues?" And my mother was struck dumb as Zechariah** was when he scoffed at an angel of the Lord who said that he and his wife would have a baby even though they were very old. My mother could not answer. Why didn't she talk about her high school as her hope for what the church could be? Why didn't she talk about Catholic anti-poverty programs throughout the Americas? Why didn't she talk about working for change from the inside out? Why couldn't she answer with any of that?

I don't know. I just know what happened next. A Baptist church around the block from us had a nursery school with a brilliant perk—curbside kid

---

* Few realize that St. Francis became famous for going out and preaching to the animals because his preaching on equality and social justice got him banned from parishes.

** Jesus' cousin by marriage once removed on his mom's side (i.e., *John the Baptist's dad*).

Ground-breaking for the new church building, a step up from the school

pick-up. You drove up, dropped your kid off, and, several hours later, he or she was standing at the curb, fully outfitted in winter wear. This meant that my mother never had to wrestle Ellen out of a car seat in a snowsuit to drop me off or pick me up. The Baptists were flat-out brilliant in their assessment of local needs. If the quality of their craft supplies was any indicator of the school, then it was an excellent program because my macaroni necklaces are still going strong to this day.

We never actually went to church there, just nursery school. But it was a step toward seeing churches besides the Catholic Church as teaching the same general principles. The nursery school broadened my mother's concept of church. She found that she was pleased enough with what I was taught there about love and justice and science and nature. She began to imagine what church life might be for the family she was building: perhaps a place where both she and my dad felt equally alien, but where their daughters saw themselves reflected in the leadership.

The final stepping stone was laid just before I was to start kindergarten, and my father's job transferred us to Texas. There, my parents were alone and exposed on the dusty plains of new construction subdivisions. Gone were the aunts and uncles and cousins and siblings who'd provided the structure for every holiday and weekend of their lives. They were truly alone.

What to their wondering eyes should appear but two couples their age with fantastic Scandinavian complexions, dragging kids in wagons around the subdivision, tucking flyers into front doors. The wholesome foursome were friends with each other from (I kid you not) performing in

Ellen and I are ready for the road derby/Easter Parade ride between our house and my elementary school where the church met (mid 1980s)

the All-American Band in the Macy's Thanksgiving Day parade together in their youth. They had decided to start a Lutheran church, and, wouldn't you know, they had kids just the ages of Ellen and me—*and* the upstart congregation was meeting in my elementary school at the end of the block.

Then an angel of the Lord descended. Kidding. But it was a heavens-opened moment in terms of providing exactly what my parents needed— a peer community. The wagon really sealed the deal. There were young families everywhere on my family's first Sunday with them—kids crawling under and between folding chairs, parents handing off responsibility in 30-minute increments for who was on patrol. The young pastor's stole was hidden behind his guitar strap. This wasn't church as they knew it, but it wasn't a bad way to meet nice people with kids.

Our scrappy, upstart community had no control of the school building where we met. The cafeteria-auditorium hybrid space always smelled of last Friday's school lunch— tater tots and Salisbury steak instead of frankincense. When the roving planetarium exhibit was installed, the pastor preached in front of black canvas with constellation patterns punched out. Many years later when I saw the intergalactic stained-glass windows in Washington D.C.'s National Cathedral, they just seemed fitting.

The bathroom and hallway lights were turned off during the summer months. Once, Ellen and me and a couple of friends all feigned having to pee at the same time, but when we got to the girl's bathroom we couldn't see anything. So Ellen stood sentinel, holding the door open to let the light in. During the consecration of the bread and wine at communion, instead of angelic bells like some churches have, our church had the "whoosh,

whoosh, whoosh" of three toilets flushing in succession. Thus, the Reformation befell the Banakis household, having far more to do with tater tots than transubstantiation.*

Our collective cells were separating and regenerating like crazy in those early days of the church of the cafeteria. During the Prayers of the People, folks would call out names of people to pray for and everyone gathered knew who the names referred to and why we were praying for their concerns or thanksgivings, and what must have happened when we went from praying for them as concerns to then praying for them as thanksgivings.

It's a mirage, of course, but that's how I remember it—church smelling of school lunch and glue, and families gathering for ridiculous talent shows and fried chicken picnics, the intimate laughter and building of our lives together from scratch.

We kept moving with my dad's job. We kept joining various churches to meet people and God. The churches I chose as an adult offered the communities I craved at the time. My college's Lutheran campus ministry was comprised of young women from public high schools in the Midwest who were majoring in religious studies, philosophy, or English—pretty specific. I joined an Episcopal Church in D.C. because it had a strong ministry for people in their twenties and thirties and because I liked the liturgy (shocking that I would choose something structured, I know) and because I supported the ordination of non-heterosexuals, a topic on which the Episcopal Church was a front-runner. My parents now attend an Evangelical Covenant church because it's where Margo discovered youth group and they found a Bible study comprised of other middle-aged people with good senses of humor.** My sister Ellen lives in a hip neighborhood of Chicago and attends an equally hip United Methodist Church that meets in an auditorium and has a professional cabaret singer leading worship. We're Christian.

In many ways, neither my mom nor my dad stopped being culturally Roman Catholic or Orthodox, respectively. The first time my father assisted at the altar for communion in the Lutheran church, he wept because it felt like such a break with his past and the Orthodox church he loved. And my mother still prays Hail Marys when fearful. She builds ritual and

---

* Transubstantiation is one of several interpretations of what happens to the bread and wine at Eucharist. Transubstantiation (standard in Roman Catholic churches) says that the elements really do become the body and blood of Christ. Eastern Orthodoxy doesn't say outright which interpretation they hold to, but they're pretty darn close to transubstantiation. Consubstantiation (Martin Luther's interpretation) says that there is real substance or real presence of Christ in the elements, but that the bread and wine remain bread and wine. Other interpretations include variations on the theme of symbolism.
** Evangelical churches are descendants of Reformation era churches and mostly define "church" as the Reformation churches did. The division tends to happen in terms of what defines an individual Christian, not in terms of what defines the church. I discuss the nuanced definition of "Christian" in the next chapter.

sacrament into daily life. They both know and honor their respective can-on of saints. The Protestant churches they ended up in merely allowed them to meet halfway, excusing themselves from traditions they loved for the sake of the family they were building together.

Would it be more honorable if my family and I had chosen churches purely based on theology and not social needs? Maybe. Would my sisters and I be better Christian adults if one parent had won out over the other and we were raised in a pre-Reformation tradition? Maybe. But we join and change churches for all sorts of reasons. And God can work with that.

I'm biased in my view. I'm being ordained Episcopal, a denomination that began when King Henry VIII of England wanted his first (of six) marriages annulled, and the pope rejected Hank's request. The king re-sponded by declaring himself the head of the church in England and the owner of the church's land, and claimed the authority to grant himself a speedy divorce. Since then, the tradition has produced some pretty great holy people, including John Donne, Madeline L'Engle, C.S. Lewis, and Desmond Tutu. God makes good things from inauspicious (and very sus-picious) beginnings.

Churches are comprised of all sorts of people who show up for all sorts of reasons. We come for friends and sobriety and cookies and an hour of quiet and help raising kids and networking. But those of us who choose to stick around are changed by one another. We pray and sing and learn and grow together. In so doing, we become formed as holy people of God.

And the church helps create good people. Each church I've been a part of has been an absolute gift. Each community has been wonderful and lov-ing, and allowed me to grow in my relationship with God, and challenged me to be a better person here on earth.

But the church is also an institution made up of broken humans. Every church I have belonged to has been riddled with pain and scandal. One pastor had an affair with the youth director. Another had class and race conflict so tangible that the air seemed to spark. Several churches had fi-nancial troubles of the tax fraud variety. One pastor's mental breakdown left the congregation responsible for everything from the sermon to the communion bread, with him stepping in only to raise his hands for the consecration of the bread and wine. More than one has been shredded by questions over women's ordination and homosexuality. The list goes on.

St. Augustine began the tradition of describing two churches or two cities—the one on earth filled with a bunch of rag-tag sinners just trying to get by, and the other in heaven full of saints and sanctity and all the sopranos singing Alleluias in key all day long.

I think, though, that maybe there are three churches. There's the pris-tine church of our collective imagination that is historically unadulterated and has never been marred by sinful motivations or human need or the society around it. That church is filled with very pretty people in simple, tasteful clothing who come to connect only to God. Those people and their leaders never disappoint one another and the children never squirm. All of the people are in complete agreement on issues of war and peace and social ethics.

Then there is the real church on earth comprised of real people trying to find community, trying our best to raise energetic children to be kind adults, trying to learn what it will mean to have a good death, singing songs off-key, enacting the sacraments, learning to forgive one another because we're still the same people coming back together week after week after week, and, in the mist of all of this, hoping to know God. In real churches, members fight against one another as they try to listen for where God is leading them in this time and place, how they will carry on the traditions of generations past. These churches are populated by people who come as much for coffee hour as they do for communion; as much in hope of finding a job or getting sober as for some mystical goal.

Then there is the church in heaven of all the saints who have gone before us, rooting for the church on earth to keep on trucking, to keep on trying to love more and learn more about what it means to be the church. They break into wild applause each time we move toward reconciliation. They cheer us on at marches and yell "Alleluia" at milestone rituals. They stick around to help clean up the kitchen on soup night and to haul the last moving box up the stairs. The saints know the struggle of being human, trying to connect to one another and to God.

In the end, that's all there is—the collective effort to know and love God better. And God is there. The bumbling attempts take place in churches of all stripes, full of real people with real histories and so many hurt feelings and disagreements. In the midst of all this reality, holiness sneaks in and makes us into *Christians*: something so much more wonderful and mysterious than anything we could do on our own.

Discussion Questions:

- What makes church "church" for you? How, if at all, does that differ from your childhood definition of church?
- Why do you come to church?
- Some people say they like Jesus, but not the church. What are your thoughts on this?
- Have you seen a church go through a scandal or been a part of one? What was it like?
- Is there ever a time for leaving a church? Leaving *the* church altogether?

12

True Believer
Who Counts as Christian

The Episcopal Church I have come to know and love and be a part of in California is, like all churches, a wonderfully odd mix. Just down the street from the Tesla Motors headquarters, it has its share of Silicon Valley venture capitalists as well as folks associated with Stanford. And yet a number of severely mentally ill people without homes are also active, pledging members of the congregation. Sandra has a color commentary reel going throughout the sermon and readings, but she's part of the congregation and never really hushed. When the donation tray comes around she drops in a wad of coins, bills, and bird feathers or lint. Phil is often found sleeping in odd corners of one of the buildings at lockup, but has the effect of dissuading other folks from breaking into the buildings or setting up shop, because he has claimed the territory. Over many coffee hours and potlucks and Bible studies, I befriend the elderly with their tales of sciatica and play Simon Says on the playground with children.

What the congregation lacks is people under forty without children—people like me. I need to look elsewhere for a Bible study or small group for people in their twenties and thirties. I've been part of a small group/ Bible study of one sort or another since my freshman year of college. There's something about praying for one another and intentionally caring for people you might not otherwise know that creates strong and deep, if somewhat ad-hoc, friendships. Bible study friends have prayed me through every job change, relationship, and move I've made over the last decade. Having that sort of small group has become integral to my spiritual life. I

need two or three or eight who gather together in Christ's name such that
he is in the midst of us.

I hit up the local megachurch to find a small group. I am a huge fan of
huge churches. Really large churches often function as resource centers for
the surrounding churches, and offer programming, curriculum, and experiences that small churches can't. My experience of enormous churches has
always been that they are insanely generous with sharing these resources
with any wandering soul who walks through the door. I am also a propo-
nent of medium and small churches. They raised me, and they offer the
intimacy that can evade large congregations.

The megachurch's worship service for people under forty is held in a
converted furniture shop warehouse. You enter the windowless room from
what had once been the service entrance where customers picked up their
sofas. The street front of the building is still retail space, now made up of
smaller boutique shops. The back warehouse area has been soundproofed
and set up with stage lighting to accommodate the full rock band that
leads the worship service. They are in heavy jam mode when I arrive. A
lovely red-haired woman bounds up to me and introduces herself as one of
the pastors. I explain that I am working at the Episcopal Church down the
street and won't be able to worship with them regularly, but was hoping
to find a weeknight small group. "Sure," she answers. "Just go online and
find an open group for the night and location you want." Can they even
dye my hair to match my gown? Jolly old town.

The service has great music and great preaching and everyone is re-
markably friendly. And attractive. I don't know if it's a virtue of the numbers game that there are more people to choose from in megachurches
and, therefore, the odds are better; or because they tend to be more engaged in modern life and, therefore, modern fashion and grooming, but
megachurches always seem to have a ridiculously attractive population,
many of whom are male. And a megachurch in Silicon Valley, where the
ratio of male programmer to female human is favorable to women? Shut
the front door.

So maybe I have a slightly ulterior motive in submitting my online
application only to mixed gender non-couples groups for people in their
twenties and thirties. *Maybe.* But when I show up at the apartment of the
host, only one guy is there anyway, and he wears a wedding ring. So much
for my grand side plan.

The apartment where they meet is decorated with crosses and scented
candles and family pictures. The group sits in a circle—some on the couch
or chair, others cross-legged on the floor. They are studying the gospel
of John, one chapter per week, with discussion questions from a shiny

pamphlet. The questions frequently use the word *believer*, as in, "How do you live out your faith in the workplace with people who aren't *believers?*"

I am not, according to the "believer" tradition, a true believer in Christ. In the early 1600s, a community of Christians spun off from the Church of England under the argument that the state church had focused exclusively on rituals at the expense of developing the faith among parishioners. The group stopped doing infant baptisms in favor of "believer's baptisms," which followed a mature confession of faith. Because of their emphasis on "believer's baptism," the group came to be known as Baptists.

Between the 1600s and the early 1800s the idea that an adult confession of faith was necessary morphed into the idea that a person needed to have a conversion experience in order to accept Christ's offer of salvation. The requirement of a spiritual conversion infused the early American Baptist and other free church* communities, as well as Methodists and many others. One churchman of this era, Nikolaus von Zinzendorf, wrote that there must be a moment when a Christian becomes awakened to his or her depraved state of existence. A true Christian must feel "the distress of our soul when we become poor, when we see we have no Savior, when we become palpably aware of our misery. We see our corruption on all sides and are really anxious because of it."[17] Only then, Zinzendorf said, are we open to accepting Christ into our hearts.

Communities today that hold with the tenet that a conversion is necessary for true faith often describe themselves as "believers" or "born again in Christ." Within those communities, the telling and retelling of one's conversion experience becomes its own sort of ritualized belief statement of how that person, as an individual, became a believer in Christ.

Margo, Ellen, and I were all baptized as infants, and then took first communion, and finally recommitted ourselves to remaining Christian as junior high students in a ceremony known as confirmation in the Lutheran church. One baptism is enough for many Christian traditions, sufficient once and for all no matter which church baptized you. The blessing of the Father, Son, and Holy Spirit is evergreen across most denominational lines. But that's not true for all churches. For believer or born again traditions, a person really needs to have a cognizant, informed experience for the born again nature of baptism to count. In Eastern Orthodox and Roman Catholic traditions, a re-baptism of sorts accompanies transferring your membership to those churches. The Lutheran church accepted my

---

* As in "local control," *free* to dictate the practice at a local level. This includes Baptists as well as a whole range of American-grown denominations such as Disciples of Christ, Church of Christ, and sometimes Congregational churches.

My confirmation with the family (Dad, Margo, Ellen, Mom), Plano, TX, mid 1990s.

Roman Catholic baptism, but the Roman Catholic church wouldn't recognize Margo's Lutheran baptism as legit. It's all very territorial.

A few years after her confirmation in the Lutheran church, Margo attended a Christian summer camp that strongly encouraged the teen campers to consider where they were in their relationships with Christ and whether they had ever really accepted Christ into their hearts. While present in liturgical churches such as Roman Catholic, Orthodox, Lutheran, and Episcopalian (among others), the question of whether you have accepted Christ into your heart is mostly found in churches that come out of the believer baptism tradition.

Margo accepted Jesus as her savior that week of summer camp. Having a spiritual experience wasn't a requirement for reintegration into the group or anything like that, but she and her peers consistently have conversion stories to tell. I believe her story, and that she had a completely authentic spiritual experience—a "warming of the heart" as the Wesley brothers* used to say. Today she and my parents belong to a fantastic small church, filled with loving people. Many of them can tell a story of coming to Christ.

I don't have a "falling in love with Jesus" story, of leaping into a relationship with complete abandon, after which everything that had been before was changed into a new, righter reality. Jesus was just always there

---

* British brothers Charles and John Wesley led an eighteenth-century movement within the Anglican/Church of England for more heartfelt preaching, singing, and emotive experiences. Classmates at Oxford dubbed John a "methodist" for how methodically and regimented he ordered his life. John took it as a badge of honor, and after the brothers died, their "flavor" of Christianity became known as Methodist.

Margo dive-bombs the baptismal font at her baptism in Hong Kong. The rest of us look on unaware, per usual.

when we were growing up. He was invited to our dinner table every night, even when we were eating out. We went to family camps together to sing songs about Jesus and retell the stories of his life. My Sunday school teachers' felt boards with cutout characters of Jesus and the disciples instructed me on the high points. My relationship with Jesus was less a story of falling in love and more a rather pleasant arranged marriage with someone who'd been hanging around the house for years.

Marriage isn't a perfect metaphor for one's relationship to a religious tradition. Jesus isn't my boyfriend. We never discuss taking out the garbage, and the Medieval mystic women's accounts of Jesus as sexual partner give me the serious heebie jeebies.* But the metaphor holds insofar as there are daily decisions along the way that comprise a lifetime relationship with the faith. My mother once remarked about my dad, "I choose to be married to your father every day." And though I'm clearly not married (see previous on scoping out hotties at the megachurch), that sort of daily recommitment makes sense to me. Whether you take your religious commitment vows at a summer camp or in a revival auditorium, or the vows are taken on your behalf when you're an infant, each day is its own choice.

---

* There were many. See, for example this excerpt from thirteenth-century poet and mystic Hadewijch who describes Christ as her beloved: "I desired to have full fruition of my Beloved, and to understand and taste him to the full... I wished that he might content me interiorly with his Godhead, in one spirit, and that for me he should be all that he is, without withholding anything from me... After that he came himself to me, took me entirely in his arms, and pressed me to him; and all my members felt his in full felicity, in accordance with the desire of my heart and my humanity. So I was outwardly satisfied and fully transported..." Um, eww.

I choose to remain a Christian today, but tomorrow I'll have the chance to reconsider.

On the drive from Chicago I had asked Margo if my lack of conversion experience made her uncomfortable.

"I just don't get it," she answered. "Why wouldn't you just make the commitment?"

"But I already did. I do. Each day I decide again to believe."

"It's different though, Kat."

Then we rode in silence.

• • •

When the pamphlet asks my Bible study believer questions, such as "How do you live out your faith in the workplace with people who aren't believers?" I make snarky responses in my head, such as, "I live out my faith by being a decent person not assaulting my coworkers with water cooler evangelism." But at the end of the session that first night, we pray for each other in the week ahead, and the next week when we return, we check in on what has happened the previous week, and I realize that if we are holding each other in prayer, I can love these folks. We can be friends.

So I become my own Federal Communications Commission censorship board; dubbing in "People of Faith" in a clumsy 3:1 substitution each time the pamphlet asks about believers. I find myself actually agreeing with the content of what people say. One of the women tells a story about flirting with a waiter at a banquet hall but not pursuing anything because he didn't "seem like a believer." That's a lot to read into, "Another mini quiche?" She only wants to go out with a "believer who has a heart for Jesus." I throw up a little bit in my mouth. Yet if asked to describe the kind of person I see myself ending up with, I want to date someone from my faith tradition who demonstrates humility, care for others, wisdom—in short, someone rather Christlike.

The more I grow to know and like the people in my small group, the more I feel like a hypocrite. Do they know that they have a nonbeliever in their midst: someone who claims to be a Christian and yet has no conversion story? What would happen when they found out?

The last time I'd been in a situation of having to tell my believer story, it was a disaster. Right after Margo and I arrived in California, I was standing outside a coffee shop, waiting for Margo to get her caffiene fix. The shop stood on the main drag of an affluent Silicon Valley suburb—full of boutiques excellent for gifts but not really practical for living. A man in a ripped T-shirt sat on the low brick wall near me, asking passersby for change. I asked how business was going that day. "Not bad," he answered and went on to explain that he actually lived in San Francisco but commuted out by bus each day to the South Bay suburbs because there was less competition. He asked if I knew where a certain church was in the city. I didn't.

"You're not from around here, are you?"

"No," I answered. "You?"

"Nope, Kansas City. But I can't go back to those winters. No place better than here if you're going to be homeless."

There was an urban legend when I worked in community development policy that when the Reagan Administration drastically cut federal funding for programs to help homeless people, shelters all across the Northeast and Midwest used their final dollars to buy plane tickets to send their clients to California. Maybe more truth than legend.

"Well, maybe San Diego," he continued. "You ever been there?"

"Once, but I was young."

"I bet you stayed in a hotel though." He was right, of course. "I stayed in their parks for a while. Real nice, but the people weren't as nice. So what do you do?"

What to say? That I work at a nonprofit? That I'm going to work in the church? I settle on saying that I'm a minister.

"Yeah? I do a men's group up at Church of the Tabernacle."

"Really?"

"Oh, yeah. So you saved by the Spirit?"

"I like to think so."

"Oh, no, sister. We got to try this again. You say it like that, people walk straight out of your church. You got to be ready to give your testimony whenever you are asked. You got to *know* you saved in the Spirit. Otherwise who'll believe your ministry?" By this time he was standing on the brick wall, gesturing wildly. He paused and then clapped once, "Sister, you saved by the Spirit?'"

"Yes?" I said meekly.

He shook his head and stepped down off the wall. "We gonna have to pray for your ministry. You got to get them in the door and keep 'em there. That's your job. Always, always be prepared to give your testimony."*

Just then Margo touched my elbow. I was saved. I introduced them.

"You saved?" He asked her.

"Yes." Margo answered without hesitation. Sell out.

---

* "Always be prepared to give an answer to everyone who asks you to give the reason for the hope that you have" –(1 Peter 3:15, NIV).

The man from the Church of the Tabernacle pointed to me as he begged Margo, "You help her with her call, please? Jesus saves, and she has to believe that."

• • •

After many weeks of learning and praying and laughing together as a small group, the inevitable happens. The pamphlet asks about our experiences of coming to Christ. The group begins a round robin of conversion testimony. I close my eyes and think of (the Church of) England.

My small group's stories are amazing in how completely unremarkable they are. Their stories are efficient and nonemotive. At some point, someone had prayed with them during a hard time, or they'd prayed for themselves for what felt like the first time. They got through the hard period and thanked Jesus for bringing them through. And the pedestrian, day-in and day-out ways in which their lives and hearts were changed are compelling. In that way, they are the holiest gospel I've heard in a while. Hell, I have those! In fact, I have rather dramatic moments. I don't have a story of falling in love, but I do have a moment when I considered the relationship and chose to stay.

Without pressure or warning, I realize that I have begun to give my testimony.

I don't have a moment when I became a Christian, I begin. I grew up in a churchgoing household (just like some of the other people in the group) and went through first communion and confirmation and all that jazz. I considered converting to Judaism in college. I was a religion major and decided that the Hebrew Scriptures had better stories.* The Jewish students on campus also had a more close-knit campus community in which many of my closest friends were active members, and a holiday devoted to the new year of the trees.** Plus, I liked the argumentative approach that the rabbinic tradition brought to scripture—debating and storytelling, generation after generation.

But there were at least two major stumbling blocks. For one thing, Judaism is a culture as much as it is a religion, and my cultural background is

---

* For example, in Judges 4 Jael, the wife of an Israelite warrior allowed an enemy combatant to enter her tent, putting Jael at risk of having her safety and reputation damaged by an enemy combatant. When the enemy combatant he fell asleep she "took a tent peg, and took a hammer in her hand, and went softly to him and drove the peg into his temple, until it went down into the ground—he was lying fast asleep from weariness—and he died" (v. 21). Hello? Awesome drama.

** Tu Bishvat or Rosh HaShanah La'Ilanot is a minor Jewish holiday, one of four "New Years" mentioned in the Mishnah rabbinic commentary. Customs include giving thanks for and eating nuts and honey and olives. It's all very Whole Foods until you get to the part where you ritually mix red and white wine, which is less gauche or gross than one might think.

in church, not synagogue. I could convert religiously, but all of my memory milestones and family life would still be Christian. I know what it is like to not really be part of the culture in which you're operating—both from moving all the time and from not really being Greek American—and it sucks. I worked retail one summer of high school and noticed as I rang up a customer that the last name on her credit card was about fifteen syllables long and ended in "ous." I asked if she was Greek. She was, and asked if I was. Then she asked where I went to church (meaning which local Greek Orthodox church). I explained that my mom wasn't Greek and that I was raised Protestant.

"Half-breed," she sniffed, and walked out.

I didn't want to spend my life stuffing my bag with Jewish cultural experiences to be Jewish enough.

Also, I suck at languages. My feeble attempts to learn Hebrew were disastrous. Not only would I be a cultural outsider, but I'd have no idea what was going on in the religious services; nor could I do any authentic textual analysis, nor could I ever do a bat mitzvah. Conversion to Judaism wasn't the best-laid plan. It's a good thing that written into the code of Jewish conversion is the requirement that you have to be turned away several times to reconsider.

Then, in the fall of my junior year at Yale, the World Trade Towers went down, and I became a person I didn't know. I sought out my largest, brawniest guy friends and huddled as close to them as possible on their extra-long twin beds to watch the newscasts. Men I had never before found attractive suddenly gave off the pheromones of fast-moving-hunter-gatherer-meets-potential-for-apocalypse-gladiator. If I could have baked them an apple pie to give them strength for their journey and insure their return home to me after the battle against whoever bombed the buildings, I would have.

At least baking would have given me something to do. But there was nothing to do; nothing to do but wait and pray Psalm 23: "The Lord is my shepherd… / You anoint my head with oil…," just like I'd learned in Mrs. Kammrath's third-grade classroom from poster boards with a cartoon drawing of a boy with what looked like egg yoke running down his face. Even though Psalm 23 is squarely situated within the Hebrew Scriptures, I prayed it in a reversion to my childhood, alternating the psalm with ardent, completely selfish prayers to a superhero Jesus. Save my life, my country, my family, my planet.

I stumbled out of my dorm and searched the sky for planes with the same intensity I normally looked for oncoming traffic. A few blocks away was a crusty stone church that always reeked of incense and pomposity. The doors were open. Over to the side was a small chapel lit by candles, and a kneeler in front of an icon of Mary. I knelt down and prayed, "Oh God, I don't even know what to ask for." I stayed until my knees went numb.

The university held classes that afternoon to give us structure. So I walked to my first day of a Christian theology seminar titled, "Evil and God: How Christian Theology Contends with the Powers of Sin and Evil." The professor began, "I hadn't planned today as an introduction to this topic, but here we are." There I was, in a class on how Christian scholars have answered the question, 'How can a good, loving, and all-powerful God coexist with evil?' I wanted to know how the faith of my childhood tried to answer these questions substantively. I wanted, I realized later, a meatier Christianity. So I stayed Christian, and so far I haven't left.

Breathless, I stop and look around the room at my small group. They smile and nod encouragingly, but no more so than they have following anyone else's testimony.

My testimony seems to suffice for the small group. Conversation moves along, and at the end we pray a little longer because we now know more about one another in a way that feels a little fragile.

I clung to my faith when the world as I knew it was falling apart. I do that all the time. When things are going poorly, I wrap myself in my faith tradition—its patterns of worship and scripture and prayers and truths I can't empirically prove. When life is going well I'm more prone to find myself like the heroine of feminist novel who can't possibly experience true growth and enlightenment in the shackles of her current marriage. She must free herself to be herself. I explore. I set out. Then life falls apart, and I crawl through the side door to find the Christian tradition still there, welcoming me back with a prayer and maybe a cup of tea. But each time, I return to Christianity somewhat changed, asking new and different questions of my tradition. I am no longer satisfied with the faith I had before and must go deeper to reconcile who I am with the faith that's been given to me.

My testimony and explanation work that week. But we aren't out of the woods. Far more had happened in my journey of confirmation and adult commitment to Christianity than I've been willing to acknowledge. Ours is a temporary peace.

Discussion Questions:

- Do you have a conversion story?
- Can someone be a real Christian without a conversion experience?
- How would you describe your relationship with Jesus (spouse/friend/ therapist/magician)?

13

Saved

The next week when we return to Bible study, one woman, who has recently gotten religion, says with such sadness that she loves everything about accepting Christ, except that her family hasn't, and she worries about them and their afterlives. Do the rest of us have these worries? Most of the group nods empathetically, much like they had with my testimony, but more solemnly. Many of them have non-Christian family and friends for whom they mourn. They too love people who can't go where they are going after death.

Each generation of Christians faces major national or world realities that call into question the truth or falsehood of the religion. Some historical event makes Christians reconsider the faith they've been given by the people who came before them. One of the events my grandparents had to contend with was the Holocaust. They had to ask how an all-loving and all-powerful God could permit the genocide of millions of innocent people. *What was God doing or thinking?* My parents faced, among other things, the collapse of faith in institutional structures following Watergate and Vietnam. *Could anything be trusted? Was every institution, including religion, a hoax?*

I maintain that one of my generation's unique experiences is that of living in an empire hub. Like ancient Rome or Alexandria or medieval Spain or Switzerland, the United States has been, in my lifetime, a place where disparate people come for work, and cross-cultural relationships ensue. Certainly the United States has always been a land of immigration, but I have cross-cultural friendships in a way that my grandparents and parents did not. Near as I can tell, a whole tangle of factors have led to my growing up with kids from many, many cultures. It's been some combination of military dominance, land acquired over generations, advances in technology and communication that made them cheap and reliable, and policies around immigration and religious freedom.

I didn't just read about Hindus or Buddhists or Muslims in Social Studies textbooks. Rather, they were my partners in doing Social Studies group projects throughout my schooling. I have personal, meaningful relationships with people from other faith traditions, and must reconcile my love for my friends and family with a faith tradition in which many have said rather loudly that only Christians go to heaven.

I mentioned in the last chapter that I went through the Lutheran confirmation program in junior high, which is when adolescents decide whether or not they want to confirm the decision their parents made to baptize them as infants. In theory, if the teen decides to confirm his or her parents' decision and remain a Christian, then he or she becomes a voting, donating member of the congregation. In reality, it's the last battle for many families in which the young persons have to go to church up through confirmation. After that, they are free to make their own choices, and it's a rare teen that either donates or endures an annual church meeting to vote on church policy. But the concept is that, in preparation for the ritual, teens are examining their faith to see if they want to buy into their parents' faith tradition now that they have some life experiences under their belts.

I had many good friends in my confirmation class at church, but none of them went to my school. My school friends were an entirely different community. I have this one memory of sitting on the floor of my friend Roxanna's house in Plano, Texas. It's summer. We're indoors to escape the heat. Her mother, Hengameh, who insists that we call her by her first name, comes and sits in a chair to chat with us. She absentmindedly picks up tweezers from the side table, and our other friend Alona crawls over and puts her head on Hengameh's lap. The conversation continues as Hengameh plucks Alona's eyebrows into an arc, patting Alona's cheek to tell her to flip sides. Then Hengameh leans down and kisses the top of Alona's head, and Alona wipes her eyes on her shirt and rejoins us in the sort of circle on the floor.

I shyly crawl over and ask Hengameh if I can go next and she smiles, "Of course!" I lay my head sideways on her soft lap. The plucking hurts a bit, but I am too excited to say anything. I have never plucked my eyebrows before, and I'm not sure that my mother would allow it if she knew.

Me and Alona (who never had braces), our freshman year of high school

She only recently started letting me shave my legs after much debate and whining. The plucking takes longer than I'd thought it would. I hope that the other girls don't notice, that they won't know that it's my first time and that it's taking longer and that Hengameh has the yeoman's task of taming my shrewish brows. Then she says quietly, "Now let me see you." I kneel to face her, and she plucks a few errant hairs. She takes my face in both her hands and purrs, "There we are, my Persian princess." And in that moment, I am, I really am Persian. I am one of hers who escaped the Khomeini revolution with her husband, a geological engineer, in the stealth of night because we were moderate Muslims. Many visa stamps later we end up in Texas because her husband found work in the oil business.

So, too, for a moment, was Alona Persian, though history would beg to differ. The facts would tell you that Alona was born to teenage parents in a fleabag hotel in Italy en route from escaping Russian Communism for the United States. The threesome would arrive in New York some months later with $1.50 in change, and share a Big Mac as their first meal. The young Russian Jewish family would move to Texas because that's where Alona's father eventually found work. Her mother would build up a real estate business helping people buy and sell all those new construction homes, and slowly they'd sponsor both sets of grandparents over. I never met a bigger Dallas Cowboys fan than Alona's father.

These were my friends, the girls I loved and longed to be loved by in the way that only junior high evokes—*I love you; I hate you; please think that I'm cool.* They were my peer group against and with whom I was developing my sense of identity and norms, because that is what you do in adolescence. And I was not about to give up my friends.

My Lutheran confirmation curriculum placed very little emphasis on heaven and hell, and much emphasis on life in the present. But I was in junior high. Hell is fascinating in junior high in the same way that horror movies are—all the blood and guts and being scared witless. So I thought a lot about hell, and it seemed like if I went through with confirmation, I was basically going to have to say that I believed that my best friends were going there, and that that was okay.

Our pastor was gruff, though he was (I'd later recognize) an incredibly capable church administrator. So I brought the question to my mother: whether getting confirmed meant that I was agreeing that I thought my friends were going to hell. My mom answered, "Maybe when Jesus says all of that stuff about 'I am the way and the truth and the life. The only way to heaven is through me,' maybe he's talking about a way of being. Your friends are good people." That became the deal I made with God. I would confirm my Christianity so long as God was cool with my friends.

The confirmation happened, and about a year later Alona and I were working on something in the drama room after school when a very bubbly, cheerful teenage girl bounded up to us, looked at Alona, and exclaimed, "Don't take this the wrong way, but you're going to hell unless you accept Jesus as your savior." There are just so many wrong ways to take that statement. Granted, the bubbly student was a very poor emissary with unfortunate methods and messaging. But even so, I couldn't imagine a lifelong faith in a tradition that condemned another child of God, particularly one I loved. For me to remain a Christian, Alona had to be allowed to remain Jewish and Roxanna Muslim without any degree of condemnation. They couldn't be pretty good, but not quite good enough in God's eyes. They had to be loved by God, period. And I realized that my greatest challenge wasn't going to be between me and God but between me and other Christians.

As often happens, I developed the vocabulary and framework years later. Stumbling upon the concept of universal salvation in my academic studies of religion was like finding that I was part of a group of people with a unique but well-documented medical condition, or discovering that I was part of secret ancestral history. So *that's* what it's called. *That's* why I've always felt this way. It all makes so much sense! Everything fits together.

Apocatastasis,* or universal salvation, asserts that what Jesus accomplished in being born a human, dying, and rising again was effective

---

* Greek: return or restore.

once and for all, and for all of humanity. In Christ, God said yes to humanity, period.

I must admit to you, gentle reader, that belief in universal salvation puts me center-left on the academic theology continuum, and definitely left of most pulpit preaching. I'm not sure that it puts me horribly far left of what many, many people actually believe in their hearts and around their dinner tables, but it's still "out there" in terms of what is usually found in print. We all like to think that we're middle class and politically moderate, but on this I have to tell you out of respect and disclosure that this puts me rather left theologically, but not beyond the pale. And, I am in most excellent company historically.

According to writings of many early Christian Fathers*—including Gregory of Nyssa, Clement of Alexandria, and Origen—all free moral creatures (including angels, humans, and devils) will share in the grace of eternal salvation. Origen wrote about this possibility:

> The end is always like the beginning; as therefore there is one end of all things, so we must understand tthat there is one beginning of all things,... from the beginning arise many differences and varieites, which in their turn are restored, through God's goodness, through their subjection to Christ in their unity with the Holy Spirit, to one end, which is like the beginning.[18]

All things are brought into unity in Christ. Augustine hated the idea of universal salvation, and it fell out of favor in the West, but it has always rumbled around in the East.

The twentieth century saw a resurgence of interest in the notion of universal salvation, especially as interfaith dialogue became the norm as opposed to the exception. It allowed a way to be engaged in interfaith work and relationships without having to think that it was a terrible pity that a wonderful non-Christian friend or family member was going to hell.

Sort of.

Some Christians who believe in universal salvation say that it's not about the afterlife at all, but rather about the heavens and hells of this life. Christians choose to live in a life with Christ here on earth because we deem it good. The afterlife is somewhat irrelevant. But I still wonder

---

* All men who died between 200 and 400 C.E. There weren't really Church Mothers publishing and making frontline policy at this time. There were fringy women living and writing out in the desert, but they weren't very mainstream. It's okay. Some of my best friends are churchmen. No, really, they are. Women began writing theology more prolifically in the late Middle Ages and haven't stopped since. Whose bright idea was it to let us learn to read and write??? Oh, wait, the church.

about what happens after death, and I hold fast to the Christian tradition of the saints throughout the ages. I love the notion that all those who have gone before us in the faith are still sort of around—in a heavenly mystical way—to give us inspiration in their life examples, and to root for us in our lives. They're dead, but not lost. We're all still connected.

Other contemporary Christians get around the heaven/hell question by saying that anyone can say "Yes" to Jesus at any time, even after human death. Think of it as an eternity of Jesus saying, "Okay, how about now?" But this interpretation means that all non-Christians must, in the timeline of eternity, become Christian in order to go to heaven. No one can stay a Hindu, Muslim, or atheist and be cool with God in the long run.

Still others say that Jesus made all people Christian, even if they don't realize it. In Christ Jesus *all* are saved, and in the fullness of time all people will be subsumed under Christ. It's like saying, "You might think you're a happy practicing Buddhist, but really I know that Jesus has you covered, so just keep yourself busy trying to crack that koan, tiger. We'll figure out who's right in the end" (*wink*). Well, that's just patronizing.

None of these quite get to the heart of what I'm dealing with, though. I don't want there to be any necessary conversion ever, either opt-in or opt-ed-in. And, so, my modern, universal salvation runs into a snaggle tooth. How can Jesus be God's real salvation for the world and not the only right highway to heaven? Christian exclusivity of salvation in Christ is incongruous with universal salvation in which there is no adoption of Christ. You can't both believe that Jesus is the way, and have God fully accept and love all people and honor their religious choices. Can you?

I just do. I live with two truths at once. Jesus is God's son and my salvation, *and* God is grand enough to truly and authentically attend to all of humanity.

Anglican theologian Marilyn McCord Adams offers one model for after-death that addresses many of these potential landmines of logic. *What if*, she says, *after the death of each person there is a big public listening session, kind of like what happened with South Africa's Truth and Reconciliation Commission, where all of the sins were confessed aloud?*

> The thoughts of every heart are revealed, so that the good deeds of the wicked and the bad deeds of the just may manifest Divine mercy, while the bad deeds of the wicked and the good deeds of the good manifest Divine justice. What we meant and what God meant during our earthly careers will be made fully explicit, so that God knows what each and every created person knows, and each knows what the others know... [T]he Last Judgment will bring full disclosure.[19]

We will each be publicly exposed and judged for who we were and what we did. How awful/ wonderful/horrible/beautiful is that? We're judged not for accepting or not accepting Christ but in the fullness of our human lives. We also are loved and forgiven for all of eternity because love, forgiveness, and reconciliation are God's true essence, which Christians believe is manifest in Christ. I love McCord Adams' model because everyone must answer to God and to one another.

Back at the believer Bible study, I am sitting in a room of people nodding solemnly with the new convert to Christianity about the fact that all of her non-believer family and friends are in for a hot future in hell. And I trot out the possibility of universal salvation. Brilliant social move, I know.

First I am met by prickly, live silence—the kind that follows violent strikes of lightning before thunder claps. Then one girl puts her rage and disbelief into words: "Never in my whole Christian life have I heard something like that. I don't know how you can claim to be a Christian and say that." Then the maelstrom of Bible bullets and doctrinal grenades begin to fall. *What about...*

- ☙ MATTHEW 10:32–33: "Everyone therefore who acknowledges me before others, I also will acknowledge before my Father in heaven; but whoever denies me before others, I also will deny before my Father in heaven.."
- ☙ JOHN 1:12: "But to all who received him, who believed in his name, he gave power to become children of God."
- ☙ ROMANS 10: 9–10: "But to all who received him, who believed in his name, he gave power to become children of God."

I sputter and say, "Let's look at the passages," but the electric air is too hot. And I would lose in a battle of Bible bullets anyway. Depending on which scholars you look to, some of these passage (and others) would support the belief that you can't accept Christ as God's salvation without that salvation being exclusive—that Christianity is the only possible right answer.

But I believe to my core that God loves my friends more than I can; that God is bigger and more beautiful than I can wrap my head around; and that God does right by all God's children. Fourteenth-century Christian mystic Julian of Norwich* wrote, "Our reasoning powers are so blind

---

* A leader of a women's religious community, she was the first verifiable female writer in the English language. She wrote extensively about visions she had of Christ. Her writings acknowledge the pain and suffering of the world without giving up a vision of God's ultimate goodness.

now, so humble and so simple, that we cannot know the high, marvelous wisdom, the might and goodness of the Holy Trinity."[20]

Jesus is my truth, my way, my window to divinity. I believe that God is all-good and knowing and powerful, and authentically revealed in Christ. But if I'd been born into Alona or Roxanna's families, I probably wouldn't have converted to Christianity, and that too would be a good and loving and right and honorable way. I don't know the details of how it all works out. That's part of the mystery of God. I just trust that it does, and that the overwhelming love of God must win.

All week I wait for an e-mail or phone call informing me that I've been asked to leave the Bible study. None arrives. I go back the next week. Still no ousting. Also no make-up platonic pillow fights, but I'll take steely silence. We continue to meet until some people marry and others move away, finally petering off by the end of the spring. Some groups exist for a transition period, and that is ours. They never kick me out. I wonder if they let me stay around because I made everyone else feel more secure in their faith. I sort of set the high water mark for heresy.

By the time the Bible study dissolves, the people in my group are more beautiful and less exotic to me than when we began. We pray for one another day in and day out for nine months. Caring and asking and knowing about day-to-day travails have a way of weaseling into the heart. They know my sadness and joy. I know theirs. Our lives look very similar, and so too, I would guess, do our hearts. Then again, I also think that Alona's heart looks very similar to my Bible study friends' hearts.

After the first couple of months, we abandon our study of the gospel of John. Sure, the pastors of their church ask all the small groups to do a sermon discussion series and then, and other interests arise. But I think it's also because, as a group, we could never get beyond John 3:16–17: "For God so loved the world that he gave his only Son, so that everyone who believes in him may not perish but may have eternal life. Indeed, God did not send the Son into the world to condemn the world, but in order that the world might be saved through him.."

We agree that Jesus saves, just not *who*. It is sad. I hope for them to be freed of fear of hell for people they love, so that instead they can love this life and the people in it, assured that God is in control forever and always. They aren't sure that I will get to heaven with my beliefs, so I may spend eternity weeping and gnashing my teeth, along with everyone else they know who isn't a Christian. Our views on salvation run on parallel but nonintersecting tracks, from the earliest theological writings straight through the present and into the future, carrying different passengers in the train cars bound for glory.

Discussion Questions:

- Is there such a thing as heaven? If heaven exists, who do you think is or isn't there? Why?
- Does universal salvation go too far to be Christian?
- Do you have friends from other faith traditions? How do they view heaven and hell?

14

Proof of Life

Resurrection

The tour guide lowers the plastic windshield outward toward the hood of the vehicle and gestures to the Macy's Women's Store on the right. We are in an awkward, metal boat on wheels. After WWII, the Navy was left with a huge fleet of tanks equipped with water propellers to move loudly and inefficiently by land or sea. These were known as ducks. The American tourism industry snatched up the galvanized metal transformers, slapped some colorful promotional magnets on the side, gave customers yellow kazoos in the shape of duck bills along with orange life vests in case of emergency and *voila*—the Duck Tour phenomenon took hold in American cities along relatively deep bodies of water. These things are made to stand out in a crowd. After all, they're boats on wheels with billboards, filled with grown adults buzzing on kazoos in the shape of duck bills. My friend Tim's visit gave me an excuse to be a tourist in the San Francisco Bay area. We decided to eat chowder sold by men in faux fisherman garb and to duck tour the Bay.

"And this is where we lose all our money. Am I right, guys?" The campy guide asks. The men around me honk their kazoos in support. "But enough of the hating," the guide continues. "In this city we know that all you need is love." Just a beat too late the guide flips on a back-up track of the Beatles, and two dozen kazoos in the shape of duck bills vibrate along with the horn section: "quack, quack, quack, quack, quack." Our kazoos and the motor drown out the excited yelps of a man in the back of the vehicle who bangs his head against the three-sided headrest of his wheelchair, knocking off a black cap that reads MIA-POW Never Forgotten.

Aunt Retz, me, and my mom, 1982

As the duck rumbles past the pricey shops of Union Square, my purse vibrates with a voicemail. I hold one finger in my ear to drown out our guide, but I can only hear snippets of my sister Ellen's message: *Aunt Retz... upsetting...thrashing...call me.* Tim leans over my lap to take pictures out the window. We aren't close enough friends for me to put my head on his shoulder, so I slump to the back of the seat to afford him a better shot, and rest my head on the rolled up plastic window rain flaps.

That morning my mom held the phone up to Retz's ear, and I said, like I always did when we talked on the phone, "Hey, Aunt Retz. It's Kathryn." And she responded "Oh!" with the same intonation she always did, but this time the "Oh" was followed by a series of mammalian noises—a dolphin or a cougar, something pre-cortex, tried to communicate, but was thwarted by the Darth Vadar rumble of a breathing machine. I said everything I could think of—that I loved sharing her birthday and her middle name and our phone calls. Mid-sentence my mom came back on the line to tell me that Retz was too exhausted to listen any more.

A week earlier I'd called from the grocery store to tell Retz about an ethical dilemma I was having at work. It was the sort of situation that if I read it in a case study I might know exactly what to do, but in the midst of living the scenario I had no idea. Retz sighed, like always, and said, "You'll figure it out kid." I usually called just to hear that.

Between that phone call and the one this morning, before the duck tour, she'd caught a late winter pneumonia, which didn't give me pause at all. She'd had congestive heart failure for years, and every six months or so visited the emergency room. She lived alone, and while her nieces and nephews stopped by her retirement community in casual rotation, the ER brought a flurry of visitors. For Retz, the ER was both medical and social.

And right now, I am on a duck tour of San Francisco, and, meanwhile, according to my mother, Retz looks like she's trying to swim. She is drowning. Her lungs are filling with fluid, and so she stretches her neck out like a turtle and kicks her legs as if trying to reach the surface where she might be able to get air. She claws at her face. A hospice consultation has been called, and Retz has begged, "Just let me go." She moves in and out of consciousness with the morphine cycles.

The duck tour lurches through a traffic jam. Our guide puts on a CD of wedding favorites, and even pedestrians, who move faster than the duck, sing and dance along to our kazooing to the Village People and Neil Diamond. My purse vibrates again. I keep buzzing on the kazoo. *What else is there to do?*

• • •

Between prayer petitions at Retz's funeral, one of the women from her retirement community gripes at full volume, "She sure picked a cold day to be buried." It is the British sort of wet, blustering cold that can penetrate rock. Wet cold lasts in Chicago until approximately July.

If we hadn't just eulogized her, I would have stepped outside to call Retz and tell her about the service. My habit of calling started sometime after I went away to college. Throughout my early adulthood I had the luxury of being far away and prodigal. I never held to a regular schedule of calling, much less visiting. So I got out of arranging her bills and pills or purchasing clothes from a niche market catalog specializing in seasonal knits with elastic waistbands. I never took a turn picking her up from the ER, or tried in vain to indicate the "Add 30 seconds" button on the microwave with brightly colored stickers when macular degeneration took her eyesight and the pigment of her irises. I would simply mention to my mother that Retz talked about eating cold soup and let the locals figure it out.

I didn't like visiting her. Between the milky white eyes, increasingly pale skin, and her disinterest in wearing dentures, Retz looked more and more like a monochromatic meth head. She was vibrant and wry on our phone calls, ageless during the daytime cell phone minutes. That's how I liked her—funny, available, and unflappably positive.

She had a habit of up-valuing her family and whatever they were doing, often for the sake of bragging rights with the women she had coffee with in the retirement home cafeteria each afternoon. I called her one January afternoon when I was living in D.C., and she asked, "The girls from coffee wanted to know if you wrote the President's whole thing or just a part?"

Aunt Retz and
Yiayia in the mid
2000s

"What?"

"You know, his thing last week."

"The State of the Union Address?"

"Yeah, whatever they call it."

"Retz, I didn't write any of the State of the Union."

"Yes, you did."

"No, I didn't."

"You told me you were working on that speech thing."

"Umm, I prepared some background charts for the mayor of New York's budget briefing. But I didn't write any part of a speech."

"Oh, well, let's not tell the girls. They'll be disappointed."

Her secret was safe. I never met the girls until her funeral reception. To try to warm ourselves, we drink tea and coffee and, in Retz's honor, scotch. My uncle raises his glass in a toast to her memory:

May those that love us, love us.
And those that don't love us,
May God turn their hearts.
And if He doesn't turn their hearts,
May He turn their ankles
So we will know them by their limping.

She would have approved. Her last words were, "Ha, ha, ha," in response to a joke my uncle was telling someone else in the hospital room when they thought Retz was in a morphine sleep.

Retz was one of my best role models for what single female adulthood could look like in all its richness. She claimed her seven nieces and nephews as her "kids," and kept up with the details of her fourteen great-nieces-and-nephews, an ever-expanding gaggle of great-great-nieces-and-nephews, and at least half-a-dozen godchildren scattered across the country. She was an easy and frequent guest, and "always had at least one spin on the dance floor."

I'm becoming a bit of a pro at being a single adult-ish female. Being on my own right after college was fun. I was living in the municipal frat house that is Washington D.C., full of young, ambitious twenty-somethings and kegs. I shared an apartment with two other girls working entry-level government jobs. We had a plasterboard wall installed down the center of our dining room to create a third bedroom so that, between the three of us, we could afford to live in a parent-approved neighborhood.

I hosted Orphan Easter for the hodgepodge of young adults living in self-imposed post-college exile. Many of the guests were actually Jewish, so the food was also kosher for Passover (eggs and potatoes in various forms). I was invited to their Seders and took far too much delight in finding the piece of hidden matzo, and they emerged from my Easter celebrations covered in egg dye. Happy, happy Zion in DuPont Circle.

Now that nearly all of my friends are paired off, I've begun to graft myself onto other peoples' celebrations. Gone are the days when a dozen folks would descend on a makeshift apartment for cheapo feasts on plastic plates. They all have in-laws, or so it seems; in-laws who gave them real plates on their wedding days.

I should be dating like a crazy woman during this bender year. But I haven't dated much this year—or the past half dozen years. Yet by no means is my fate sealed. I've known happy couples who marry up into their eighties, and I have, possibly, another ten years to have biological children. With each of my friends' weddings I attend, though, I do wonder, "Will it ever be my turn?"

If my fellow clergywomen are any indicator, dating once ordained is brutal. Young male pastors get snatched up like hotcakes, but there's no "sexy priest" effect for women in clerical collars (*other* collars, perhaps, but not clericals). Female clergy work evenings and weekends in androgynous uniforms, and we cannot, under any circumstances, date congregants. Such behavior is immediate grounds for defrocking.* It's absolutely *verboten*, and with good reason.

I could date other church employees, but the demographic composition of the church workers I know in major metropolitan areas is approximately that of a Cher concert—middle-aged women and gay men of all

---

* Being unordained or decommissioned as a minister, not literally stripped. Disappointing, I know.

ages. The clergy demographic is more hetero-male nationwide, but in the circles I run in, one has to clarify which Madonna is being talked about.

It's not just my profession, though. My being single is mostly me. It's been me working out who and where and how I want to be as an adult. It's been about giving in to a calling to work in and for the church when very few of my friends are religious. It's finding ambitious tasks more compelling than the slow work of relationship building. It's been me wanting to do things such as move across the country and change careers and put myself through school to say that I could, so that if everything fell apart tomorrow, I'd still have done all those things.

The single life isn't a prison sentence. I dance at every wedding, even if it's just me and the flower girl out there shaking it loose. I've never spent a holiday alone, and I don't anticipate I ever will, if only because I know to gird my loins* and ask to come along somewhere a few weeks before the holiday and to always, always do the dishes. I try to blend in and make myself useful. But sometimes I do want to reach over and grab a hand under the table.

I used to call Retz when the longing for a partner set in deeply. I'd call to tell her about waking up in the middle of the night, alone, to the mewing cries of mice caught in an obstacle course of glue traps set around my apartment, and putting on three layers of rubber gloves to dispose of their vermin remains. She'd laugh and laugh, and, eventually, so would I. But now she's gone.

I attend my parents' church the day after Retz's funeral. Their bubbly pastor begins the service by asking us to close our eyes and picture the face of someone we knew who doesn't "know the awesome love of Jesus." I stare at the ceiling and picture nothing—not a face or a situation or story from the news. I don't even bring to mind the face of someone I was really annoyed at, the way I sometimes do in a passive aggressive way, as in: *So-and-so is an awful person who needs the love of Jesus, unlike me.* The awesome love of Jesus is complete bullshit right then, unless the awesome love of Jesus were to appear in the form of a quiet soul with a bottle of scotch, who would hold my hand and gently say the only phrase really acceptable for a sympathy card, which is, "Oh, wow. That sucks."

My parents ask me about my Easter plans as we drive to O'Hare. I answer honestly: *I don't know.* For the first time in recent memory I'm not among other single young adults; nor am I working Easter weekend in a church, because I'm not on staff. I am in limbo all the way around. I

---

* The term "gird one's loins" was used in the Roman Era, meaning to pull up and tie ones lower garments between the legs to be able to run faster. Now it just means preparing for the worst.

haven't planned ahead and have nowhere to go. They suggest I call up our old friends from Hong Kong with the really beautiful house not far from where I live. The ones who read the Bible somewhat differently than I do. *Good idea,* I say, convincing no one.

• • •

My coworkers give me the wide berth we afford those who mourn, and avoid eye contact my first day back to work. The ethical snarl I'd called Retz about hasn't been resolved, but I lack the emotional reserves to deal with it. The grief goblin steals my brain to the point that all I can do is read articles online and send personal e-mails, including one e-mail to the friends from Hong Kong, asking if I can crash their Easter celebration. They call right back to tell me that I'm more than welcome to come, and (great news) they'll be having Easter at their daughter's apartment because she's just had an emergency C-section.

I can't imagine anything I'd want less, as a first-time mother covered in stitches down under, than a surprise visit from a childhood friend. I rescind my invitation request. I even call a second time to give them an out. The husband argues with me, "You're part of our tribe. We want you there." I believe him, enough. I am so grateful that he's argumentative.

Two embossed, enormous invitations to friends' weddings greet me in my accumulated mail. The two envelopes bring out inverse *schadenfreude**—I am saddened by their good fortune. I am going to have to put on heels and a dress and seem happy for my friends' good fortune in finding partners when I have nary a prospect.

I collapse against the kitchen doorframe and hold my stomach and make a sound I can only describe as keening. From somewhere behind my gut I moan all vowels.

I know this moment. It has happened before.

I am back at my studio apartment in D.C. with the huge peephole and vermin infestation. In the pee-scented hallway, I have just opened up my final law school rejection letter, and I have stepped smack onto one of the glue traps in my entryway. A few weeks ago I broke up with a very good man who had said, "Just tell me what to do, and I'll do it," but there was no "it" to change, just two people who weren't compatible. Most of the friends who came over for Passover Orphan Easter had moved on to grad school or to other cities, and I hadn't been on the same exodus timetable.

---

* German: to take pleasure in another person's misfortune.

I drag the trap with me to the doorway separating my bedroom-living room from the molding bathroom, and I collapse in the doorframe, shouting, "You'd better have a fucking plan, because this sure wasn't mine." A dark dotted line—flax seeds smuggled from my kitchen cabinet, interspersed with the oblong black pepper grinds of mouse droppings—weaves across the bathroom counter, right next to my toothbrush.

The evening in my kitchen in California adheres onto that night in D.C. and becomes an authoritative reality. Despair does that. Anguish does that. Guttural emotional pain does that. They knit one pain to another so that everything that might happen in between is subsumed as a foolish, whimsical aberration.

Real life, Despair says, is hurt and loneliness. I can barely recall a run I took in the Santa Cruz foothills just before Retz caught pneumonia. The fog was low enough that I was running above the cloud line, and every now and then the sun would burn through, and I'd see that I was above a green valley. I giggled with delight and said aloud, "Amen, sweet Jesus!" because that's what I say when awed.

Despair corrects me now, "Stupid girl. You thought that that was some sort of sustainable reality? Not for you. Remember Easter that year of the mice? You were rejected from law schools and single, and everyone seemed to have moved on to better lives. That was the year Ellen came over and dragged you to brunch at a little creperie, and you wanted to crawl across the cast iron bistro table and right into her lap. *That* is your norm. Your real, sustainable life is the days you have to be put together with toothpaste and safety pins."

My constitutional predisposition is toward moments when I collapse in doorways and can't form sentences and blow my nose on something pulled out of the hamper.

I yearn for vice. I want cigarettes that will send my brain buzzing and let me focus on the elemental fascination of fire devouring dry wood. I want booze or pot. I'd even settle for a pressing work deadline to focus on. I want anything that will flood my brain and body with chemicals that might release me from this grip of pain, even if the chemical rush is temporary.

In D.C., I turned on the bath water and swabbed the counter with bleach wipes and poured myself a glass of red wine while the tub filled. The heat of the bath would push me into a woozy sleep faster. In California I clutch at my belly until I hear the two little girls who live upstairs playing outside on the patio. I hush myself because I don't want to scare them. My bones are poured out like water, as the psalmist says, and somehow it is my fault.

• • •

In the midst of sadness I cannot remember recent kindnesses, like the fact that one of the girls who just sent out wedding invitations woke up before dawn on her birthday to drive me to the airport to fly to Retz's funeral. I cannot recall any of the three years in between that evening in D.C. and now. Only the two moments of deep sadness connected in a masterful and nearly impenetrable *trompe l'oeil*.*

I cannot see forward to fifteen minutes later, when I'll sigh and stand up and wash my face and flip on the radio and start chopping vegetables for dinner. I cannot predict the next day at work, where I'll process our quarterly expenses and counsel a high school student on his college application essay.

I cannot envision the next session of the adult ESL class, where I volunteer, falling on April 1 and the teacher trying to explain the pseudo-holiday in Spanish:

Teacher: April first is a day of jokes.

Student 1: Telling jokes all day?

Teacher: No, doing jokes.

Student 2: Funny ones?

Teacher: Not always.

Student 1 again: A whole day?

The teacher then throws his hands up and returns to the pirate chant of possessive pronouns in the second and third person, "Your, her, your, her, your, her."

And it is impossible for me to imagine Easter will be when God sends unseasonably cold and relentless rain, and there is nowhere to go but to my childhood friend's apartment, as we eat ham off of paper plates propped on our laps, sit knee-to-knee, and pass around a new human with miraculous toenails who already has a signature move of making a surprise "O" face that slays us all. The proud grandfather, who reads the Bible differently than I do, bear hugs everyone within arm's reach all afternoon long, just bursting with joy. His wife makes sure that I have my very own Easter basket, which means that they made a last-minute shopping trip just for me.

I sit to the side, as Retz would have done, chatting and telling stories—but mostly listening and becoming enmeshed in this holy people of God.

---

* French: "deceiving the eye" or "an optical illusion." It's a painting technique to make something appear 3-D.

There is nowhere I would rather be than flooded in with this family, grafting myself onto their sides. The author of 1 Peter writes to a community in pain and in fear, and renames them: "Once you were not a people, but now you are God's people." Days before, I had forgotten that I was part of the fabric of God's family, and now I am part of this gracious people of God once again.

That is how resurrections happen for me sometimes. They—the people of God—hover and wait until I trust that they're real.

The character of Thomas in the gospel of John gets a bad rap because when Jesus appears to the other disciples after having been killed days before, Thomas isn't there, and doesn't believe their witnessing, and says he won't believe until he can put his hands in Jesus' wounds. Thomas requires a sensory proof of life before he can believe that Christ is present with him and risen. I do, too.

There are many who find the concept of Christ's resurrection, particularly a bodily resurrection, superfluous. For them, whether Christ was raised from the dead or not has no bearing on their sense of faith.

There are others who interpret the way the disciples saw the resurrected Christ as something akin to how dead loved ones sometimes come to us in dreams in startling real ways, so that when we wake up we're rattled with how authentically we've encountered them.

But I'm with Thomas. I need to touch and taste and see that the Lord is good and present. I believe so easily in sadness that I need very, very bodily proofs of the resurrection in order to hope and believe in the Christian project.

Our temporary lives and bodies matter. Our blood and bones, fluids and solids ground us in this world. They are what make us the living. Someday we will not be. We will transition over to something else—spirit, dust, darkness, heaven—but for now we're here. We are alive in this physical world, the same physical world of physical bodies that Jesus inhabited. And I need the very earthly stuff of smell and taste and touch and sound that brings me back to this life and body. The stuff of this world poses the possibility that pain doesn't have the last word.

Resurrection dawns on little cat feet, and it sounds like a pirate pronoun chant and tastes like Cadbury eggs and smells like a newborn's head and feels like a rib-crushing hug from a proxy father and looks like San Francisco drizzle coming straight down. Hope saturates me from every angle, and I begin to believe that Christ is risen once again.

Amen, sweet Jesus.

Discussion Questions:

- When, if ever, have you experienced grief? What was it like?
- Do you remember a moment of coming out of grief?
- What do you think happens after we die?
- What are your thoughts on Jesus' resurrection? Does it matter whether it was physical or spiritual?

15

Conclusion

And then, without much warning, I'm back in the Chicago area, unemployed and living with my parents, like so many other young adults. I go on informational interviews as if it's my job, which it sort of is. After the second or tenth or twentieth informational interview, I notice something happening. Every interviewer compliments my resume with the same phrases. Their kind platitudes start to feel like a PTA mom giving me a high-five after a "Rudolph" solo in the second grade holiday concert. Then the interviewer asks why (on earth) I quit my job in California and moved to the Midwest in the midst of a recession. Family, I respond. It sounds cagey, like maybe I really needed a kidney donor or accountability in rehab. No one digs any deeper because legally they really shouldn't, even in an informational interview.

I don't explain anything about flying back and forth for Yiayia's funeral, then Thanksgiving, then Christmas, then Retz's funeral all within a few months—only to end up at our family friends' for Easter and thinking, "I have a family, one I quite like. They all live in one place. I could spend all of my money and vacation days in other ways if I lived near the family I love."

I also leave out the part about attending the shower for one of the embossed invitation brides and keeping a spiral notebook list of all her gifts and thinking, "I could be single among my married friends and cobble together a community with them and their in-laws, or I could be single with my own family."

The interviewer inevitably concludes the meeting by assuring me that some organization will snap me up. Then he or she reaches out a hand to shake. I extend what has reliably been my right hand, only to find it harder and harder to close my fingers around the proffered one.

Some small bone seems to disintegrate into calcium powder as we shake. Another interview, another metacarpal turned to dust. "Thank you for your time," I whisper, pulling back what had been my hand but now feels like a silicon sac with five tributaries. I hold the hand sac as I skulk to the borrowed car, staring at the pavement.

Along with the bones of my hands seem to go degrees of skin pigmentation. I become less and less visible to myself. When I apply my make-up in the locker room of the YMCA, all I see are the red lockers behind me and the women around me getting dressed for their work days. My own reflection disappears into the multi-color-to-the-point-of-drab industrial carpeting and other people.

Other un-dead unemployed begin to appear out of the camouflage of coffee shop furniture and library walls. They sometimes offer a furtive nod before hunching back over their laptops and spiral notebooks and that single, small cup of black coffee that pays for their hours of sitting unnoticed. Many wear hats, perhaps to shield their faces from the light that has become dangerous to their almost translucent skin.

I hunger for the blood of meaning and purpose. People who say they cannot wait for retirement have social lives and savings plans and jobs they only sort of resent. They have never sputtered to articulate who they are and what they can do into months of untimely unemployment. We, though, slide through public libraries like grey jellyfish in ball caps. I look forward to weekends when so many more people mill out about aimlessly and give the air a hum of humanity.

More disturbing than the loss of the use of my hands or my skin tone is the loss of my words. Each cover letter I send into the abyss takes some of my words with it. My brain starts to stall. I sit with a stack of bright white job openings in one pile on my left, and various versions of my resume and old cover letters on my right, and I cannot take the steps to combine them. The descriptions of scope of work, the ideal experiences and skills for candidates, and the coy "compensation commensurate with experience" statements leave me stammering.

I know that I should read the job description and circle the key words like "manage" or "independent" or "multitask" and then make sure to include them in my cover letter. Great job-hunters craft their resumes to highlight the employer's priorities and select relevant references. A diligent applicant cyber-stalks an organization to try and learn as much as possible about the place of work and, ideally, the hiring manager. I should try to find a connection between myself and that place. I just can't. My brain refuses to connect the words on the job description with the words of my past, my former self who managed a budget and staff and tried to invent a twenty-fifth hour in the day to get done all I wanted and needed.

From the days when I began writing scholarship applications to try to pay for college, I've relied on my ability to convince strangers to trust me with money. As a lobbyist and then as a fundraiser, I wrote letters and e-mails and white papers to get strangers to give me lots and lots of funding even though we didn't know each other. When it comes to the issue closest to my heart—me—I can't string words together to get them to pay me.

The longer I send out letters and go on interviews, the more intimidating the job descriptions become. I've always had trouble with typos, and over time any job description that dictates attention to detail seems outside my capabilities—even though I have done plenty of technical, detailed work in the past. I don't want to oversell myself when there are so many people applying who presumably never confuse *they're*, *their*, and *there*.

I even lose my nice words. Well-intentioned friends and family ask how my job search is going, and I can't answer. E-mails pile up in my inbox. I don't want to answer until I can say that I have an offer, so I just don't respond. One friend calls for an unrelated reason, but makes the mistake of asking if I'd heard back from a recent interview. "When I hear something good, you'll be the first to know," I snap.

Certainly other parts of the world have known this existential fear in a palpable way from generation to generation. A bright, promising, child in Southeast Asia or Russia or Africa or Central America might not have believed that hard work would lead to an interesting job or a house or a better life than the one he or she knew. But I had a little touch of Manifest Destiny sprinkled on my breakfast cereal. I grew up believing that the horizon was limitless if only I kept working hard and pushing on. Yet here I am with all my fancy degrees and experience, and there is no work to be had. What am I to say to that? How can I find meaning and purpose without the probability of steady employment? What do you do when there is no more land to be conquered and tamed, no more bullish market to be held by the horns?

After three promising rounds of interviews, and writing samples, and discussion of pay and benefits for a grant writing job that I would just love, I receive a form letter rejection in the mail. I had built up a whole dream world of exactly which trains I'd take to commute each morning, and how I might have to change trains when winter arrived. The park filled with homeless and retired persons across the street from my office would be my secret lunch spot on sunny days.

I call Emily in California to spew over the phone in the illogical, fatalistic way I do. *What the freak am I good at? I can't get a job. And I can't write a "pay me" letter for myself, so how could I expect people to pay me to get money for them? I have no friends because I have just moved back. Why on earth did I move back to the Midwest? What was I trying to prove? I will never be able to write another cover letter and will never be employed.* Also, maybe I don't trust in God's providence enough, so I am a super sucky person of faith.

My voice sounds, even to me, like the end of the book of Jonah, when the prophet has been sparring with the Lord and refuses to do the Lord's bidding and walks into the desert where the compassionate Lord provides a tree for shade. But Jonah responds in a voice I always hear sounding like the lead character in *Napoleon Dynamite*:

> The Lord God appointed a bush, and made it come up over Jonah, to give shade over his head, to save him from his discomfort; so Jonah was very happy about the bush. But when dawn came up the next day, God appointed a worm that attacked the bush, so that it withered. When the sun rose, God prepared a sultry east wind, and the sun beat down on the head of Jonah so that he was faint and asked that he might die. He said, 'It is better for me to die than to live.' But God said to Jonah, 'Is it right for you to be angry about the bush?' And he said, 'Yes, angry enough to die.' (4:6–9)

Is it right for me to be angry and paranoid and pissy? Yes, angry enough to die.

Wise, patient Emily listens to my voice crackling through the cell phone. After I run out of ranting, she asks, "Hmmm, I just wonder... I wonder how it is that you want to remember this time in your life?"

I answer, "As little as possible."

"I'm serious," she persists. "If you knew that this period would end at some point, how would you want to be able look back on what you did with that time, especially after your year in California?"

How do I want to remember this time?

Maybe I want to remember it as a post-resurrection story, because overall it was fast and weird and left me blinking and confused like the stories of Jesus' resurrection left his friends. One minute Jesus is alive and teaching. The next minute he's dead. Everyone is distraught, and then three days later he's having a fish fry on the beach (in the gospel of John), disguising himself as a person who doesn't pay attention to the news (Luke), meeting his disciples at their designated emergency evacuation spot (Matthew), crashing a dinner party with bad news (Mark). The end. The gospels are all buildup of teaching and mystery, then the execution, then just a snap-shot of the resurrection, and then they're over.

The resurrection accounts are even shorter and odder in the context of all of the rest of the Bible. The Hebrew Scriptures (many more pages than the New Testament) are full of stories of a coming messiah for generations upon generations. Then there are the four short gospels about a charis-matic rabbi who some claim to be the Son of God, but no one is quite sure. He's killed and rises again very quickly. The gospels are followed by the much longer non-gospel material of the New Testament, which discusses how the nascent Christian communities begin to process what happened in the resurrection and how their lives have been changed by it.

It's almost as if Jesus' life, death, and resurrection didn't happen at all—except they did, or so I choose to believe.

A similar speed and strangeness characterizes my last several weeks in California.

One minute I am taking over Megan's life and apartment, and the next minute she is on her way back from Russia and needs her worldly posses-sions back, and I am quickly plugging all the holes in her walls to hide evidence of the pictures I've hung.

• • •

One minute I'm hoping that the bishop of Connecticut will send me to the Dominican Republic, and then next minute I'm calling him for a consultation on my ethical quandary at my office. We agree that while the answer isn't clear, I need to separate myself from the situation and look for a new job. He remarks, "I'm sorry you've had to go through this situation, but I'm glad for the church that you've been exposed to these things early on in your ministry." He explains that because I've seen the effects of this situation in one workplace, I'll be on the lookout for it go-ing forward. The church is never immune from the situations any other organization faces.

• • •

One minute I'm aghast that Vid's wife doesn't play games. The next minute she and I are driving home from the bachelorette party of a mutual friend, and I am whining about the fact that I have to provide games for the same bride's upcoming shower. Vid's wife with the beautiful hair and smile probes, "Why do you hate wedding showers so much?" She herself has just gotten married in epic, Indian fashion the year before.

I lose my façade of decorum and my ability to take my audience into consideration, and rail that weddings are needless because people are getting married later, they're money pits, and…I'm afraid I might never have one.

She stays quiet for a moment and then says, "I'm afraid I'll never be able to keep up with all of you from Yale. You're all so smart."

"You're as smart as any of us are," I argue back.

"When you all get together you're smart differently. What I can bring is cookies."

The more I get to know her, the more I like her. She's like me—fragile.

• • •

One minute I'm talking to Yiayia about her car. The next minute I'm watching a man with grease on his hands secure her old, blue sedan to a tow ramp with industrial nylon straps. He asks if I need anything else, pointing to the tax write-off receipt in my hand. I shake my head and move behind a shrub to continue a commendation ceremony as the body of the car is raised and lowered with chains and straps into its final resting place. It seems silly to say prayers for the dead for a car, but I do anyway.

• • •

One minute I'm gainfully employed in a community with perfect weather and ample friends. The next minute I am George Costanza from *Seinfeld*—long-since graduated from college, unemployed, and living in my parents' basement. I'm a parent's nightmare—two degrees from a fancy pants school, voluntarily unemployed during a recession, uninsured, and surfing the Internet in my childhood bedroom. Nice.

• • •

Yeah, maybe I'll tell it as a resurrection story because, just as the disciples thought they knew Jesus—"*BAM!*,"—this wild thing happened and they realized that the Messiah and his ministry looked different. This guy they'd hung out with was the Messiah and the bread of life, and they'd have to carry on the mission differently. I thought my life was going to go one way, and then things changed really quickly and I saw my world and ministry differently.

Maybe it's a uniquely generational and situational story, a snapshot of a world in change—the way every generation is.

29 YEARS OLD

MY MOM	ME
Married to my dad	See K. Bolick, "What, Me Marry?" in *The Atlantic*
Has amassed savings	See itemized bill from the education loan company ED Financial Services for two rounds of higher education debt
Bought and sold several homes	See Housing and Urban Development on homeownership
Moved up the ranks of Chicago-based corporation, until…	See U.S. Bureau of Labor Statistics on employment in domestic based corporations
Has baby and chooses to stay home	See U.S. Census "Birthrate Continues to Decline." See also U.S. Bureau of Labor Statistics, re: working mothers
Active member of civic organizations	See R. Putnam, *Bowling Alone*

No, no, no…it's not unique at all. It's just a classic coming of age story of a girl realizing she wanted a life and family in the Midwest all along. I move all over the country only to realize that I want the hallmarks of what Yiayia and Retz had—multiple generations of kin at arm's length with whom to share life's joys and sorrows and cleaning the gutters and Easter dinner. I pray for a husband and children of my own, but living with family is not dependent on those variables. I have a great, big, fat extended family already. And for all the ways that my mother's and grandmother's and aunt's lives at twenty-nine were different than mine is, there are still strong similarities. We all want to live good lives, read good books, have good relationships, leave the world better than we found it, and spend our time doing something well that feels meaningful.

Except…let's theologize it. It's an apocalypse story of a girl going somewhere new and different that forces her to examine her life and her call to ministry and her family differently. But just like Dorothy in the *Wizard of Oz*, she sees her call and her family differently when things return to normal. In the alien terrain she learns that she was never alone or lost at all, and she draws on that memory ever after.

No, no, maybe it's a story about how we make meaning in the midst of our years here on earth, regardless of the outside forces. "We have time," wrote theologian Karl Barth. "Threatened though we may be, we are not in time in such a way that it continually slips away into infinity and is therefore lost forever. Time is. It is the form of man's existence, the form of our existence. To be man is to live in time."[21] We are given these lives to craft as we will, to choose to say "Yes" to God and frame our time together, or not.

We get this one life to make meaning with God and with one another. Barth writes, "There is no part of our time which is not as such also His. It is, so to speak, embedded in His eternity. But as we are thus in God's time, He limits ours."[22] And in between we choose how we live out our lives together and how we see our stories and lives wrapped up in God's.

In the end, all we have are our stories. We Christians are a storied people. We tell our biblical stories and family stories and morality stories and conflict stories again and again, interpreting them in the light of who we are here and now. We read into them and extract out of them differently in each reading or telling. And there is always so much more.

Discussion Questions:

- Have you ever job searched? What was it like?
- What has been something that was bigger than you could handle alone?
- How would you cast or describe the story of your life with God? How would you have told it a few years ago?
- Has your life ever come around full-circle, so that you were back in a place you thought you'd left behind? How were you different when you returned there? How were things different around you?

Epilogue
I Am an Astronaut Fireman

round 2 a.m. I start having nightmares of M.C. Escher*-style disappearing pews, my subconscious freaking out about the one thing
I needn't worry about—that people wouldn't have anywhere to
sit. The church where I've been hired to work 10 hours a week was built
just a little too late. The second half of the 1800s witnessed two parallel
movements in Episcopal Church history. Domestically that period was the
population high water mark for Episcopalians in the United States, both
in percentage of the population at large and presence in positions of power.
The 1880 General Convention of the Episcopal Church included fifteen
past, present, or future members of the U.S. House and Senate. We've
since ceded that distinction to the Mormons. (You're welcome.)

Since then we've been on a steady population decline, but we've got
spirit. The same era was a time of rapid and robust international missionary zeal. By the time construction began in earnest on St. Luke's Church
in Evanston, Illinois, in 1906, both movements had started to wane, but
the blueprints remained large enough to bring all people to Christ within
that single building's stone walls.

Happily, the charismatic leader who built St. Luke's had enough per-
sonality and presence to fill the room. The vestments made for George
Craig Stewart, who was first a priest and then the bishop of the diocese of
Chicago, are pieces of embroidery and textile art that would make Liberace

---

* Dutch twentieth-century graphic designer who did spiral staircases and the two hands drawing each
other. You'd know his stuff if you saw it.

swoon. Museums call every now and then to ask if they can borrow and display the stoles (straight up and down neck scarves priests wear when preaching), chasubles (a tablecloth-like garment with a hole in it that a priest wears when doing communion), and frontals (table cloths for the altar) made during his time. Thanks to dietary and genetic realties of that era, Stewart was only 5'4", so all of the vestments fit me to a tee.

The room where clergy go to put on vestments is decorated with three stained-glass panels commemorating Stewart. One panel depicts him preaching from the pulpit as listeners lean forward to hang on his every word. The next shows a phalanx of young boys holding his vestments as he begins the communion service. My favorite is the tableau of "the poor" (evident from their raggedy hair, torn clothing, missing limbs, and general heroin-chic effect) being restored and healed by his very proximity. Just to the right of the window triptych is a small prayer altar in front of a mural, which looks innocuous enough—some random Renaissance picture of the holy family in pastel tights—until you look closer and realize that it's the holy family plus Stewart (also in pastel tights), who is holding up a wee little stone church on a pillow. You too can pay him homage.

Fast forward to my ordination, a service for a single person in the twenty-first century, an era when all mainline churches are in an Escher-like riptide of disappearing population and identity. Having enough seats in an Episcopal church is never a problem. But do I have nightmares about elderly guests not being able to find bathrooms or parking, or problems with the vinyl camping pergola we've jury-rigged over the pipe organ to protect it from falling limestone? *No.* My psyche fixates on the pews.

Though I arrive two hours before the service is set to start, the building is already alive with people showering me in their love languages. The retired funeral director I've asked to coordinate the reception after the service is throwing around tablecloths and terms of endearment. Later, when a friend of mine asks where the bathroom is, she will take my friend by the hand and lead her right to the door. Our wiry, male master of ceremonies is doing a final spacing walk-through for the bishop's chair and other props up front, his mustache twitching in thought. Between our rehearsal last night and now, he's found a table to replace the one that was discovered to be broken at the rehearsal.

A piano tuner pings away. Our organist is truly world class, but she decided that one of the hymns I've picked out would sound better with piano accompaniment than organ, so she has voluntarily humbled herself to play the piano instead of her mother tongue during just that hymn.

Slumped in sleep in the back pew is an Afghani teen whose family has been sponsored over the years by a parishioner couple. He is majoring in

videography at the local arts college and has been strong-armed into film-
ing and editing the service to fulfill some assignment or make some cash,
perhaps both.

They are all here, and many others follow, to allow me just to be me
for the day. Not hostess, or master of ceremonies, or artistic coordina-
tor—just me.

I flit. I pace. I reposition. I've taken the last week off from the consulting company where I work full time so that I can be very Zen and centered
for this day. And I am. Zen and centered with a shot of adrenaline and
built-up anticipation. My Blackberry is locked in a desk drawer so that I
can't send snarky e-mails to coworkers at my day job.

A year and a half ago, deep in the bowels of my job search, I one day
forced myself to e-mail everyone who had been gracious enough to give
me an informational interview. I described how I had employed the advice
that they gave and asked if they had heard of any openings since we'd met.
One friend of a friend of a friend of a friend who worked at a fundraising
consulting firm e-mailed right back and said that his firm had an opening,
but I probably wouldn't want it. It was mostly doing tech support calls for
their in-house software. I'd be fielding the same angry client complaints
over and over and running interference between the programmers and the
users. Plus, it was a for-profit company, and I probably didn't want that.

Oh, but I did. It was a salaried job with health insurance. The friend
by many degrees of separation was a serious witness to me of God's grace
when he coached me through what to say to which person during the interview process. At the end of the marathon, the hiring manager looked at
me and said, "I was expecting to hate you, but you don't suck." It's been an
open marriage made in heaven ever since. My firm knows about my other
life at St. Luke's in Evanston, and the church knows about my work with
the firm.

St. Luke's was once a huge, flagship congregation in the area, with a
world-renowned choir. So, when the empire fell, it was real big and real
ugly and real public. Long story short, in the late 1990s/early 2000s a
sordid meltdown resulted in the head priest and the music director both
leaving with sizeable severance packages and several hundred parishioners.
The congregation became an instant classic seminary case study of how to
deal (or not) with congregational conflict and disaster. Think Tylenol post-
poisoning in the 1980s.

But they were rumored to be on the upswing, thanks in part to the
leadership of a tough, smart, innovative head priest named Jeannette
who preached with a William Shatner smirk. They had an opening in a
part-time position they called the "community connector," with a vague,

rambling description of using community-organizing principles to help newcomers get involved in the congregation.

I went to worship there one Sunday without introducing myself to anyone, really. The building was a spectacular stone structure that felt like some European cathedral. Jeannette's preaching was smart and challenging. But what really got me was coffee hour (always my favorite thirty minutes). Stranger after stranger came up to me and remarked something to the effect of, "We're just trying to find out what it means to be church in the twenty-first century. Maybe we'll be in this building. Maybe we won't. We're trying to figure out what the Holy Spirit is saying now." They had gone through a process of discerning whether to close, sell the building, partner with other organizations, move, or something else. In the end, no one wanted to buy a building with a century of deferred maintenance in a real estate crash. Who knew? But it was the process of considering their own demise, their own ceasing to be, that galvanized the congregation into something new, flexible, and well. Sometimes I think that we work together because when we met, the congregation led with the statement, "Hi, we've thought about not existing," which allowed me to say, "Oh, good. I've considered not being a Christian, much less a priest, and have spent time being very sad and angry." Having looked over the precipice, we're freed from fear.

Around 588 B.C.E. Jerusalem was sacked by the Babylonians.* It was ugly. The Israelites who survived the attack had to figure out what it meant to be an ethno-religious community without having their own land or temple or anything like that. As I left St. Luke's that first Sunday, I called a seminary friend and yelped, "I have met the holy remnant of Babylon. They are in Evanston."

Within a few months, Jeannette went from being a rumored decent priest in the diocese to a person I'd donate a kidney for if she needed it and a person I'd be so happy to grow up to be. And, as happens, I began to fall in love with my new parish. So began the dance of "multi-vocational ministry"/"clergy with a day job"/ "living as multiple selves at once."

For a while I was obsessive about shielding one community from the other. But I am a lousy adulteress, though a pretty decent polygamist. I try to erect Chinese walls in terms of funding streams and time allocation, but each of my communities knows about the other. And there is inevitably crossover. Many colleagues know some of the parishioners, and some *are* parishioners, which keeps me honest.

Sometimes I have to step into an office with a door that closes at work to take a pastoral call, and sometimes I have to leave church meetings

---

* Many of the best-loved prophets of the Hebrew Scriptures wrote about or during this period.

because our software has crashed at work. Most of my week is spent at my day job, and I have the luxury of being able to preach about challenges with my clients and colleagues. When my parishioners and I plan projects, we face the same time constraints, which, in turn, set our expectations of one another. The Mondays after I preach, or following high holy days, I arrive at my day job looking like someone released from a failed clinical trial for narcolepsy treatment, but I've also been able to listen closely and deeply enough to our clients over time to develop new, profitable products for the firm. Both of my employers are insanely accommodating and flexible and kind.

Some days I resent one job or the other, or the whiplash of switching between them, but mostly not. Most days when my alarm goes off and I curse at it, I think, "What would I rather be doing? If money were no object, would I rather be not working at the firm or at the church or anything else? Would I rather be sipping a mai tai in Tahiti?" The answer is *no*.

I'm doing exactly what I want to be doing. I love all of my jobs, and I don't have to choose. I am an astronaut firefighter.

• • •

My ordination really is the prom scene at the end of the teenage romantic comedy, except real. Just before I go to line up in the processional, I run into my third grade teacher from Hong Kong who would shuttle us outside during bomb threats. She lives in another Chicago suburb now, and found out about my ordination from my mother's Christmas letter. When I express amazement at seeing her, she just shrugs and says, "I am part of your heritage."

My heritage this day is vast and varied. By the time I begin to walk down the aisle, the old stone building is packed. The incense bearer leads a procession of choir and clergy past the CEO and many of my colleagues from the firm that pays me, past Eva and Emily and her husband Matt, and Megan, and Vid and his wife, and so many other people who have played Trivial Pursuit in my living room. The family friends from Hong Kong who had me to dinner at their California home when I first moved in and then to Easter dinner when I couldn't stand up straight are there too. I see a fellow lobbyist from D.C. whose basement I lived in after the mouse infestation waves. And throughout the crowd are all of my big, fat, Greek-Irish-blended aunts and uncles and cousins, and, of course, members of the congregation.

At the front end of the church, my bishop, the one who has shepherded me through this process, turns and faces my presenters and me. He asks if

Solemnly swearing before my bishop, the wonderful Right Reverend James Curry as the MC looks on

I have been selected according to the church's rules and regulations. The priest at the church where I interned in Connecticut and a member of St. Luke's both answer that I have. Then he asks the gathered congregation if I am fit and if they will support me in my priestly ministry, and they agree so loudly that my eyebrows shoot up.

"The Examination" follows. I stand before my bishop in stilettos, on the shoulders of giants—the matriarch Sarah who laughed at God and lived to tell about it, the patriarch Jacob who wrestled a blessing out of the angel but was never the same after that, Augustine and Aquinas, all the early church fathers, the medieval mystics, Barth and Rahner, and all of the saints who have gone before me and affirm without irony:

> I solemnly declare that I do believe the Holy Scriptures of the Old and New Testaments to be the Word of God, and to contain all things necessary to salvation; and I do solemnly engage to conform to the doctrine, discipline, and worship of The Episcopal Church.

We sit, and one of the women who dragged the little red wagon down our street in Plano, Texas, gets up and reads a bit of the book of Numbers about how Moses shared his leadership with seventy others in the desert. She's followed by a friend from Hong Kong who has memorized a passage from Philippians so that she is looking directly at me when she says,

> Finally, beloved, whatever is true, whatever is honorable, whatever is just, whatever is pure, whatever is pleasing, whatever is commendable, if there

is any excellence and if there is anything worthy of praise, think about these things. Keep on doing the things that you have learned and received and heard and seen in me, and the God of peace will be with you. (4:8-9)

A choir of child sopranos chants, "You have searched me out and known me... Your works are wonderful and I know it well." There is nothing like the sound of children singing to break your heart. Adult sopranos sometimes populate the suburbs of hell, but good child sopranos are spectacular, and these kids are really good.

Jeannette climbs up into the old, crotchety stone pulpit and tells me, "You must bring your whole self to your ministry." By the time she steps down I am a hot mess of mascara and snot because, really, that is what I've been running from during this whole book, that my whole self was unacceptable for the life of faith, and certainly not appropriate for church leadership.

The bishop asks me a few more questions, and then he calls the clergy in the assembly to come forward and gather around me. I kneel in the midst of them, and the choir begins a chant, "Veni Sancte Spiritus,"* and slowly the gathered assembly joins in, timidly at first. It goes on and on, with descants sung and played by an oboe over the top, on and on until we're all in rhythmic trance, invoking the Holy Spirit.

In the sparkly silence that follows, the bishop places his hands on my head and pushes down hard, so hard I'm not sure what to do with the concrete slab below that will not yield. All of the gathered clergy put their hands on me, just as others did at their ordinations, creating a symbolic and spiritual (if historically questionable) chain back to the disciples, back to Jesus our great high priest. The bishop prays, "Therefore, Father, through Jesus Christ your Son, give your Holy Spirit to Kathryn; fill her with grace and power, and make her a priest in your Church."

Because, at its best, religious ritual or sacrament is an outward sign of an inward transformation, that is what happens. I become a priest in Christ's church.

My parents and sisters drape one of Stewart's most resplendent chasubles over my head so that I am "vested according to the order of priests." Familiar fingers loose my hair from the neck hole of the vestment. I know those hands. They have held my head since before I could do so myself. My parents and my sisters are endorsing me with their very beings and bodies.

In the end, my ordination as a priest doesn't feel like a change, like I'm something or someone different. There is no sense of having magical

---

* Latin: "Come, Holy Spirit."

My first act
as a priest,
declaring the
peace

powers. Rather, it feels like a public moment of transparency. Finally, everyone in my life knows that everyone else exists. There is no secret life.

There is laughing, crying, hugging, eating, and skipping about—and also anointing with holy oil and consecrating the Eucharist—all great elements for a celebration.

And, after, we all get on with the business of living out our baptisms. It's a good life.

Notes

1. *The Book of Common Prayer*. New York: Church Publishing Incorporated, 1979. Print. pp. 304-305.

2. Calvin, John Institutes III.ii.29,30 in *Joannis Alcini: Opera Selecta*, ed. P. Barth and W. Niesel, v. 3. Munchi: Kaiser, 1928., 39.1-40.12, quoted in Alister Mc-Grath's *The Christian Theology Reader*. Third Edition. Malden: Blackwell, 2007. Print. 446

3. *Book of Common Prayer*, 370.

4. Barth, Karl. *Church Dogmatics*. VI.2. Edinburgh: T&T Clark, 1956. Print. 138.

5. *Commentaries on Romans and 1-2 Corinthians (Ancient Christian Texts)*. Translated by Gerald Bray. Downers Grove: Inter Varsity Press, 2009. Print. 13.

6. Pascal, Blaise. *Pensées*. Parish: Editions du Seuil, 1962. Print. 198, quoted in McGrath, 34.

7. Carson, Anne. "Putting Her in Her Place. Woman, Dirt and Desire." In *Before Sexuality. The Construction of Erotic Experience in the Ancient Greek World*. Eds. David M. Halperin, John J. Winkler, Froma I. Zeitlin. Princeton, NJ: Princeton University Press, 1990. Print. 154.

8. BV 118 *VS*, and *Iliad* 14.165 quoted in Carson, 137.

9. Jobs, Steve. Text of Stanford University Commencement Address, 2005. Stanford Report. 14 June 2005. Web. 28 October 2011 (http://news.stanford.edu/news/2005/june15/jobs-061505.html) Web.

10. Rahner, Karl. *Foundations of Christian Faith: An Introduction to the Idea of Christianity*. New York: Crossroads, 2006. Print. 121.

11. Rahner, Karl. *Theological Investigations Volume VI: Concerning Vatican Council II*. Baltimore: Helicon Press, 1969. Print. 222.

12. Most everything I say about the definition of apocalypse is thanks to New Testament scholar Barbara Rossing in her wonderful book *The Rapture Exposed: The Message of Hope in the Book of Revelation*. New York: Basic, 2004. Print.

13. Landau, Yehezkel. "The President and the Prophets" *The Jerusalem Post*. Nove, 1983, reprinted in *Christianity and Crisis* as "The Predient and the Bible," Dec. 12, 1983 and quoted in Rossing, 90.

14. Quoted in Lee Griffith, *War on Terroirsm and Terror of God*. Grand Rapids: Eerdmans, 2002 and Rossing, 10

15. *Journey to Adulthood*. Leader Resources. (www.leaderresources.org). 30 December 2011. Web PDF download. pp. 36–37.

16. Leo the Great, *Sermon* 95 de natali ipsiusi; in *Sources Chretiennes* v. 200, ed. Dom Rene Dolle. Paris, Cerf: 1973. P. 266. Quoted in McGrath, 497.

17. Von Zinzendorf, Nicolaus Ludwig. *Nine Public Lectures On Important Subjects in Religion*. Tranlsated by George W. Forell. Iowa City: Univerity of Iowa Pres, 1973. Print. 40-41. Quoted in McGrath, 458.

18. Origen, *De principiis*. 1.6.2. Translated by Paul Koetschau. London, Society for promoting Christian knowledge,1936. Print. 53.

19. Adams, Marilyn McCord. *Christ and Horrors: The Coherence of Christology*. Cambridge: Cambridge University Press, 2006. Print. 238.

20. Julian of Norwich, *Revelations of Divine Love*. London: Penguin, 1998. Print. 85.

21. Barth, Karl. *Church Dogmatics*. V3.2 London: T&T Clark. 1960. Print. 521.

22. Ibid

from The Young Clergy Women Project

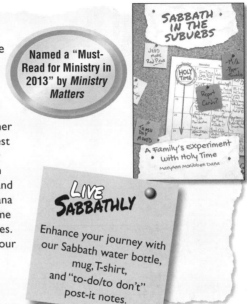

Sabbath in the Suburbs
A Family's Experiment with Holy Time
by MaryAnn McKibben Dana

Named a "Must-Read for Ministry in 2013" by *Ministry Matters*

Sabbath-keeping seems quaint to many in our 24/7, twenty-first-century world. But the Sabbath isn't just one of the Ten Commandments; it can transform the other six days of the week. Join one family's quest to take Sabbath to heart and change their frenetic way of living by keeping a Sabbath day each week for one year. With lively and compelling prose, MaryAnn McKibben Dana documents their experiment with holy time as a guide for families of all shapes and sizes. Each chapter includes tips to help make your own Sabbath experiment successful.

9780827235212

LIVE SABBATHLY

Enhance your journey with our Sabbath water bottle, mug, T-shirt, and "to-do/to don't" post-it notes.

Any Day a Beautiful Change
A Story of Faith and Family
by Katherine Willis Pershey

Rocking a newborn. Loving an alcoholic. Praying for redemption of a troubled relationship. Groping in the dark for the living God. Katherine Willis Pershey's story of her life as a young pastor, mother, and wife is at times hilarious and harrowing, and it reminds us God is always with us.

9780827200296

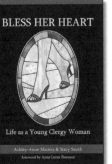

Bless Her Heart
Life as a Young Clergy Woman
by Ashley-Anne Masters & Stacy Smith

What does a pastor do on a date? How should she announce to the congregation she's pregnant? How does she establish her pastoral identity when a congregation isn't used to a female in the pulpit? The personal issues a female pastor faces may be far different than those her male counterparts face, and a congregation's reaction can be far different too. Ideal for women in ministry or considering a ministerial calling, *Bless Her Heart* presents real-life, first-person scenarios from pastors in a variety of denominations, church sizes, and ministries.

9780827202764

www.chalicepress.com • 1-800-366-3383

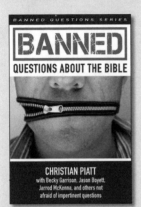
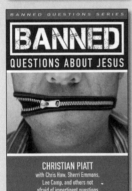